Leonhard Schmitz

A History of Rome with a Map of Italy and Ample Chronological Table

Leonhard Schmitz

A History of Rome with a Map of Italy and Ample Chronological Table

ISBN/EAN: 9783337380052

Printed in Europe, USA, Canada, Australia, Japan

Cover: Foto ©ninafisch / pixelio.de

More available books at **www.hansebooks.com**

Authorized Text-Book Series.

A

HISTORY OF ROME

FOR

JUNIOR CLASSES.

BY

LEONHARD SCHMITZ, LL.D.

CLASSICAL EXAMINER IN THE UNIVERSITY OF LONDON.

WITH A MAP OF ITALY AND AMPLE CHRONOLOGICAL TABLE.

Canadian Copyright Edition.

TORONTO:
COPP, CLARK & CO., 47 FRONT STREET EAST.
1878.

Entered according to Act of the Parliament of Canada, in the year one thousand eight hundred and seventy-eight, by COPP, CLARK & CO., Toronto, Ontario, in the Office of the Minister of Agriculture.

PREFACE.

This little History of Rome has been drawn up for the purpose of giving the young student a brief but fair picture of the origin, growth, development, and decay of the Roman state. The early or mythical period, which has been passed over entirely by at least one modern historian, could not be altogether omitted in a book of this kind, partly because legendary tales are always specially attractive to the imagination of the young, partly because they show in what light the Romans themselves viewed their own early history, and lastly because, though the mythical or legendary character may be fully admitted, they nevertheless contain many traits revealing to us the social, religious, and political life of the early Romans, not to mention the fact that a knowledge of those legends is absolutely necessary to understand the numerous allusions to them which we meet with in the poetical productions of modern nations.

The later centuries of the Roman Empire, subsequent to the reign of Commodus, appeared unsuitable for very young people, for with few exceptions it is only a history of wretched and contemptible despots, containing little that can benefit or elevate young minds. Hence that part of the history has been briefly characterised only in a few broad outlines, showing the rapid decline and final dissolution of the once mighty fabric of the Roman Empire. It is hoped that this little volume, like its companion, the "History of Greece for Junior Classes," may be found a suitable introduction to the study of the larger Histories of Rome which have been produced in this and other countries during the last fifty or sixty years.

L S.

LONDON, *August,* 1875.

CONTENTS.

	PAGE
INTRODUCTION,	9

CHAPTER I.
From the Foundation of the City of Rome to the Establishment of the Republic, B.C. 753 to B.C. 509, . . 12

CHAPTER II.
From the Establishment of the Republic to the Legislation of the Decemvirs, B.C. 509 to B.C. 451, . . . 29

CHAPTER III.
From the Decemviral Legislation to the final Subjugation of Latium, B.C. 451 to B.C. 338, ... 39

CHAPTER IV.
From the Subjugation of Latium to that of all Italy, B.C. 338 to B.C. 272, ... 52

CHAPTER V.
From the Conquest of all Italy down to the Outbreak of the Second Punic War, B.C. 272 to B.C. 218, . . 61

CHAPTER VI.
From the Second Punic War down to the End of the War against Antiochus, B.C. 218 to B.C. 188, . . . 71

CHAPTER VII.
From the Peace with Antiochus down to the Time of the Gracchi, B.C. 188 to B.C. 133, ... 80

CHAPTER VIII.
From the Time of the Gracchi down to the First War against Mithradates, B.C. 133 to B.C. 88, . . . 89

CONTENTS.

CHAPTER IX.
From the First War against Mithradates down to the Death of Sulla, B.C. 88 to B.C. 78, ... 99

CHAPTER X.
From the Death of Sulla to the Outbreak of the War between Cæsar and Pompey, B.C. 78 to B.C. 49, . . . 106

CHAPTER XI.
From the Civil War between Pompey and Cæsar down to the Battle of Actium, B.C. 49 to B.C. 31, . . 117

CHAPTER XII.
The Reign of Augustus, B.C. 31 to A.D. 14, . . . 128

CHAPTER XIII.
From the Death of Augustus to that of Nero, A.D. 14 to A.D. 68, ... 134

CHAPTER XIV.
From the Death of Nero to that of Domitian, A.D. 68 to A.D. 96, ... 142

CHAPTER XV.
From the Death of Domitian to that of Marcus Aurelius, A.D. 96 to A.D. 180, ... 148

CHAPTER XVI.
The Reign of Commodus, A.D. 180 to A.D. 192.—Conclusion, 154

CHRONOLOGICAL TABLE, ... 158

INDEX, ... 166

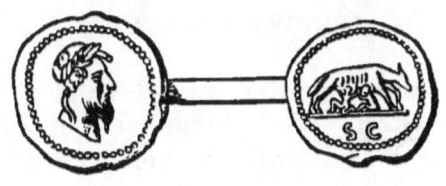

A ROMAN COIN.

HISTORY OF ROME.

INTRODUCTION.

The history of Rome differs from that of most other nations, inasmuch as it is the history of a single city, which, at first small and insignificant, gradually extended its dominion and imposed its laws not only upon Italy, but upon nearly the whole of the ancient world. The city of Rome throughout the whole period of Roman history was the heart and centre of the Empire; and a more gigantic system of power centred in a single city, the world has never seen. As she extended her conquests, she at first also extended her constitution, though in a modified form, to the conquered peoples who were admitted to her franchise; but this plan was soon given up, and the conquered nations were reduced one after another to the condition of subjects, having to bear all the burdens of the state, without enjoying the privileges of citizens. Such a system was fraught with very many dangers, and ultimately led to terrible wars by which the city was forced in the end to concede the rights of citizenship to the whole of Italy.

Rome was originally one of a number of small towns in Latium, a district on the west coast of Central Italy, and its inhabitants of course were Latins. These Latins again were only one of the many tribes inhabiting the whole of Central Italy, all of them closely allied to the inhabitants of Greece, as is still manifest from the great resemblance subsisting between the language of the Greeks and the dialects of the nations of Central Italy, especially the Latin, which is the best known among them. This resemblance is in fact so great that it is clear there must have been a time when the Greeks and Italians were united as one nation speaking the same language. The Central Italians, therefore, as well as the Greeks, belong to the great Aryan family of nations, who immigrated into Europe from the East; and on their arrival one branch occupied the peninsula of Greece, while the other proceeded to Italy, which they appear to have entered from the north. In their new country they again separated into several branches which became afterwards known by the names of Umbrians, Sabellians, Latins, Oscans, etc., and whose languages differed from one another only as dialects.

But besides these Central Italians, we meet in Italy with other nations, such as the Etruscans or Tuscans, at first occupying the plains of Lombardy, but afterwards settled in Tuscany or Etruria, which derives its name from them. They appear to have been pushed southwards and across the Apennines by swarms of Gauls descending from the Alps and conquering the country between those mountains and the Apennines. The south-east of Italy, moreover, was inhabited by a race called Iapyges, probably the earliest immigrants into the peninsula, who had been pushed to the southern extremity by subsequent immigrants. The most recent inquiries have shown that all these nations, including even the Etruscans, about whom so many wild conjectures have been formed, belonged to the Aryan race.

But in addition to these, the southern coasts of Italy were covered with Greek colonies, whence that part of the peninsula is sometimes called Great Greece (*Magna Græcia*). Hence, in spite of all appearances to the contrary, the whole of Italy, including Etruria and Cisalpine Gaul, was inhabited by nations belonging to one and the same great race, whose original home appears to have been in the north-west of India. Their arrival in Europe, which must have been very gradual, and have occupied a long period of time, may be assigned in a general way to the year 2000 before the Christian era.

PLAN OF THE CITY OF ROME.

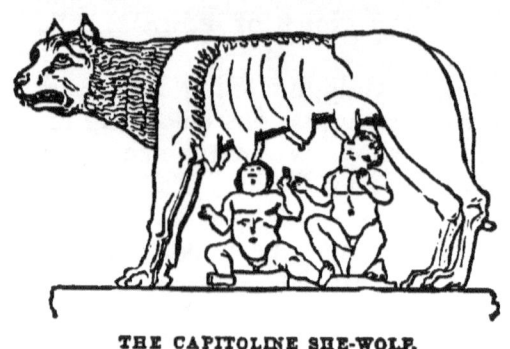

THE CAPITOLINE SHE-WOLF.

CHAPTER I.

FROM THE FOUNDATION OF THE CITY OF ROME TO THE ESTABLISHMENT OF THE REPUBLIC.

B.C. 753 TO B.C. 509.

In treating of the earliest history of Rome, we must bear in mind that we are dealing with mere legends, as is the case with all other nations whose history pretends to go much further back than their written literature. In the case of Rome the legendary, or, as we may call it, the artificial character of its early history may be inferred all the more from the fact that in the year B.C. 390, when Rome was taken and destroyed by the Gauls, most of the ancient historical records perished, and had to be restored as far as possible from oral traditions and legends. This legendary part might therefore be passed over altogether, were it not that the legends were believed by the Romans themselves, and are so much interwoven with the subsequent literature not only of the Romans, but of nearly all the nations of Europe, that it becomes a necessity to have some general knowledge of them. Moreover, although the events themselves recorded in the legends may have no historical foundation, they yet enable us every now and then to catch a glimpse of the social, moral, and religious condition of the people, or at least of the light in which the Romans themselves viewed their early history, which itself is a matter of no small interest. We shall therefore give a brief outline of the earliest or legendary history of Rome, adding, where necessary, a few remarks pointing out what must be regarded as fable, and what may be supposed to convey some historical truth.

The story about the foundation of Rome runs as follows: *Æneas*, one of the Trojan heroes, is said after the destruction of his native city by the Greeks, to have arrived in Italy with a number of followers, to have founded the town of Lavinium in Latium, and to have thus become the ancestor of a long line of kings. *Ascanius*, his son and successor, founded the city of *Alba Longa*, which henceforth became the seat of government, and is said to have been the head of a confederacy of thirty Latin towns. *Procas*, one of its last kings, at his death left two sons, *Numitor* and *Amulius*. The former, being the elder, succeeded his father, but Amulius rebelled against his brother, drove him from the throne, and in order to secure his unjust possession of it, ordered the son of Numitor to be put to death, and then compelled the daughter, Rhea Silvia, to become a vestal virgin, whereby she was obliged to remain unmarried. But by the god Mars she became the mother of twin sons, *Romulus* and *Remus*. Thereupon Amulius caused her to be killed, and her infants to be thrown into the river Tiber. The river at the time happened to have overflowed its banks, so that after a short time, when the waters subsided, the basket containing the babes remained standing on dry land. There they were suckled by a she-wolf, and fed by a woodpecker, until they were found by the shepherd, Faustulus, who took them to his wife, Acca Laurentia. When the boys had grown up to manhood, they distinguished themselves by their bravery and their noble bearing; by an accident they became acquainted with their own history, and with the assistance of their comrades drove Amulius from his usurped throne, which was now restored to their grandfather Numitor.

This being accomplished, they resolved to build a town on the Palatine hill near the spot where they had been saved. When the new town was finished, a dispute arose as to which of the two brothers should give it its name; from words it came to blows, and Romulus slew his brother. In order to increase the number of inhabitants, Romulus opened an asylum, inviting all and sundry to come and settle in the new place. Vagabonds of every description came, and all were welcome. But as there were no women among them, the population would soon have died out, and in order to prevent this, Romulus applied to the neighbouring communities of Latins and Sabines to obtain wives for his subjects. This request was scornfully rejected, and Romulus then resolved to obtain by a cunning device what had been refused to his fair demand. He invited the neighbouring tribes to a festival to be celebrated in honour of the god Neptune; and while the strangers were witnessing the games, the Romans suddenly seized their daughters and carried them by force to their homes. To avenge this outrage, the Latins and Sabines took up arms against Rome. The former were easily defeated, but during the heat of the fight with the Sabines, the Sabine women threw themselves between the combatants, imploring them to desist from destroying one another, and declared themselves willing to remain with their new husbands. A peace was then concluded, in which it was agreed that the Romans and Sabines should thenceforth form only one state, but that each nation should retain its own king. The Sabines then under their king, *Titus Tatius*, built a new town for themselves on the Capitoline and Quirinal hills, near that of the Romans. The two nations for a time lived in happy peace and concord; but not long after, Titus Tatius was killed during a sacrifice at Lanuvium, after which Romulus alone reigned over both Romans and Sabines.

Soon after this, Romulus became involved in wars against Fidenæ and the Etruscan town of Veii, in both of which he was successful, the Veientines being even compelled to give up a portion of their territory on the right bank of the Tiber. After a reign of thirty-eight years, from B.C. 753 to B.C. 716, he was removed from the earth in as marvellous a manner as that in which he had come into it; for one day, while he was reviewing his troops, his father Mars descended in a tempest and bore him up into heaven. He was ever after worshipped as a god under the name of *Quirinus*, and regarded as the guardian and protector of the city he had founded.

Such is the legendary account of the life and reign of Romulus; but the Romans at all times looked upon him not only as the founder of their city, but also as the author of the groundwork of their political institutions. Hence he is said to have divided his people into three tribes, the *Ramnes*, *Tities*, and *Luceres*, each tribe into ten Curiæ, and each Curia into one hundred gentes or clans. The senate or council of elders, originally said to have consisted of one hundred members, was increased to two hundred, when the Sabines or Tities (from Titus) were incorporated with the state. The Luceres, however, were certainly not formed by Romulus, but were added at a later time when the senate was increased to three hundred members, which for a long time after remained its normal number.

Besides the sovereign people thus organised into tribes, curiæ, and gentes, there existed in the earliest times two other classes, the clients and the slaves. The former were retainers of certain families or clans, and the person to whom a client was attached was called his patron (*patronus*, from *pater*, a father), which shows that the relation subsisting between a client and his patron resembled that between a father and his son. The plebeians, or the commons of Rome, did not exist in those early times, unless the clients be regarded as plebeians, as is done by some historians.

After the death of Romulus, a whole year passed away without a successor being elected, and in the meantime the government was conducted by the senate. At length the Ramnes or Romans chose from among the Sabines

Numa Pompilius of Cures, a man renowned for his piety and wisdom. The legend represents him as the founder of all the great religious institutions, just as Romulus is described as the author of the political organisation of the state. Numa's reign was a period of uninterrupted peace, during which the people were engaged in the peaceful pursuit of agriculture and in the worship of the gods. In all he did the king was supported by the counsels of the nymph *Egeria*, with whom he had interviews in a sacred grove near Aricia. The first thing he did was to build a Temple of Janus, which remained closed throughout his reign, a sign that Rome was at peace with all her neighbours. He then instituted the several orders of priests, as the *flamines*, priests devoted to the special service of the gods Jupiter, Mars, and Quirinus, the *vestal virgins*, and the *salii* or dancing priests of Mars. He next appointed the college of *augurs* (*augures*), consisting of four members, whose business it was to ascertain the will and pleasure of the gods by observing the flight of birds in the air and their manner of feeding. The college of *pontiffs* (*pontifices*), lastly, consisting of four members, headed by a fifth called the *pontifex maximus*, possessed most extensive powers in all matters connected with religion. After having thus regulated religion and all its numerous rites and ceremonies, Numa Pompilius died after a reign of forty-three years, from B.C. 715 to 672.

The story of this king is quite as mythical as that of Romulus; the religious institutions ascribed to him had no doubt existed among the Latins and Sabines from time immemorial, as is clear even from the legends about his predecessor. The religion of the Romans, like that of the Greeks, was only an offshoot of the religion of the great Aryan race, and consisted originally in the worship of the various powers manifested in nature, such as the sun, the moon, the heavens, and the earth, with the various forces displayed in them. But in later times that simple worship of nature was corrupted by foreign influences, especially by the mythology of the Greeks, for the Romans themselves had scarcely anything that can be called mythology.

After the death of Numa Pompilius the Romans chose *Tullus Hostilius*, who belonged to the Ramnes, for their king. His reign, extending from B.C. 672 to 640, is described as the very opposite of that of Numa, for he is said to have neglected the worship of the gods and to have been engaged in perpetual wars with his neighbours. The first of these wars was waged against Alba Longa, in consequence of certain acts of violence for which reparation was refused by that city. The contest between the two little states remained for a long time undecided, until at length the commanders arranged that the dispute should be determined by a combat of three Roman brothers called the *Horatii*, with three Alban brothers called the *Curiatii*, who happened to be serving in their respective armies; and it was agreed that the conquering party should rule over the vanquished. When the three champions of each party met, two of the Horatii were killed, while all the three Curiatii were indeed wounded but still able to fight. The surviving Horatius then took to flight, and the three Curiatii pursued him at such intervals as their wounds permitted. This was what Horatius had foreseen, and turning round, he slew them one after another. It was thus decided that Rome should rule over Alba. When the Romans returned home in triumph, Horatius met his sister, who burst into tears and lamentations, when she saw among the spoils won by her brother a garment she had woven with her own hands for one of the Curiatii, to whom she had been betrothed. Horatius, enraged at her conduct on such an occasion, ran her through with his sword. For this outrage he was tried and sentenced to death; but he availed himself of his right to appeal to the people, who, moved by the recollection of what he had done for his country, and by the entreaties of his father, who by his death would have been left childless, acquitted him. This tragic story is unquestionably no more than a popular tradition or a poetical fiction, but the fact of Alba having been overpowered by the Romans and become subject to them need not on that account be doubted.

The people of Alba, however, bore their subjection to their neighbour with great reluctance, as was shown very soon after, during a war of Rome against the town of Fidenæ, in which the Albans, who were bound to support Rome, formed the treacherous design of joining Fidenæ, if the Romans should be worsted. The treachery, however, was discovered by Tullus Hostilius, who, after successfully terminating the war, ordered the commander of the Albans to be put to death, and their city to be razed to the ground. This order was immediately carried into execution, and the Albans are said to have been transferred to Rome, where they were ordered to settle on the Cælian Hill. Some of the most distinguished Alban families obtained all the rights of Roman citizens, while the great body of the conquered people entered into a relation which was neither that of full citizens nor of slaves. They were called the *plebs* or *plebes*, to distinguish them from the old Roman citizens, who were called *patres*, *patricii*, or *populus Romanus*. The power of Rome was thus doubled by the fall of Alba, and the Roman king now waged a fresh war against the Sabines and Latins, over the latter of whom he claimed the same authority as that previously exercised by Alba. But the king's victories were of little avail, for by his neglect of the worship of the gods he had incurred their anger, and he and his whole house were destroyed by Jupiter with a flash of lightning.

After his death, *Ancus Marcius*, a Sabine from among the Tities, and a relation of Numa Pompilius, was raised to the throne, which he is said to have occupied from B.C. 640 to 616. He at once set about to revive the religious institutions, which had been neglected by his predecessor, but he was unable to devote his whole time to them, for the Latins, who had concluded a peace with Tullus Hostilius, thought that they might assert their independence under a peace-loving king like Ancus. He was thus obliged to resort to war, in which he displayed no less vigour and energy than Romulus and Tullus Hostilius. Many of the Latin towns were taken, and some were destroyed, and at last the whole force of the Latins was defeated in a pitched battle near Medullia. Many thousands of them also were transferred to Rome, where Mount Aventine, and the valley between it and the Palatine Hill, were assigned to them as their habitation. These new settlers entered into the same relation as that of the conquered people of Alba—that is, they became plebeians, whose number must now have far surpassed that of the old citizens or patricians. These plebeians had no share in the assemblies of the curiæ, and were consequently excluded from the sovereign rights of their conquerors; but they were personally free and independent of the patricians. Considering their numerical superiority over the patricians, and the fact that there were among them men of influence and power in their former homes, such a state of things could not last long. It is further probable that a great many of the conquered Latins did not migrate to Rome, but remained in their old homes on their estates. Ancus is also said to have drawn Mount Janiculus within the city, to have connected the two banks of the river by means of a wooden bridge, to have built the port town of Ostia, and to have established salt-works at the mouth of the Tiber, whereby the Roman dominion was extended to the sea.

The reigns of the last two kings are most remarkable, because they form the period during which Rome obtained its commonalty, for thus the plebeians may be called. They form the most interesting part of the Roman population, for they never ceased struggling to remove the disabilities under which they were suffering, and to obtain as much power as was necessary to protect them against the arrogance and oppression of their patrician conquerors.

It is a curious fact that the legends represent the first four kings of Rome as alternately belonging to the Ramnes and Tities—that is, to the Latin and Sabine tribes—no king of the Luceres being mentioned.

The remaining three kings are said to have been foreigners, and the legends describe them as having come from Etruria. The first of them, Tarquinius Priscus, is described as a descendant of a Korinthian, Demaratus, who is said to have emigrated from Korinth, and to have settled in the town of Tarquinii, in Etruria. The sixth king, Servius Tullius, is in some traditions described as an Etruscan, but considering the liberal spirit in which he framed a new constitution for Rome, it appears more likely that he was of Latin origin.

It is further remarkable that the Roman state, which under Ancus Marcius is said to have comprised only a small portion of Latium, suddenly appears under his successor as a great monarchy, under which great architectural works are constructed, some of which remain down to the present day.

The fifth king, *Tarquinius Priscus*, who is reported to have reigned from B.C. 616 to 578, is represented, as already remarked, as a foreigner, who by his wealth and wisdom gained the favour of Ancus Marcius, and thereby succeeded in raising himself to the throne as his successor, to the exclusion of the sons of Ancus. One of his first acts was to increase the number of senators by one hundred, so that henceforth that body consisted of 300 members. It does not seem improbable that the increase in the number of senators was connected with the incorporation of the tribe of the Luceres with the state. In order further to increase his power, he undertook a war against the Latins, in which he was so successful, and brought home such splendid spoils, that out of them he was enabled to celebrate games more splendid than those of any of his predecessors. For this purpose he is said to have laid out the great race-course for horses and chariots, called the *Circus Maximus*. He then became involved in a war with the Sabines, and finding that his cavalry was insufficient, he doubled the centuries of cavalry, so as to raise their number to 1800. By this means he was enabled thoroughly to defeat his enemies. During these wars the Etruscans are said to have supported the king's enemies, for which Tarquinius chastised them in two successful battles; after which the Etruscans are reported to have submitted to the Romans. But what makes his reign still more illustrious are the great architectural works which he executed, such as the great sewer (*Cloaca Maxima*), whereby the Forum and other low districts of the city were drained, and which still exist in an almost perfect state of preservation. His foreign origin seems further to be attested by the innovations he introduced into the religious affairs of his people, for it was in his reign that the gods were first represented in human forms. He began the building of a temple of Jupiter on the Capitoline Hill, and he is further said to have intended to surround the city with a stone wall, which, however, was prevented by his wars, and to give to the plebeians a kind of organisation.

The two sons of Ancus, who had always considered themselves wrongly treated by Tarquinius, when they learned that he had determined to leave the throne to Servius Tullius, his son-in-law, hired assassins to murder the king. But his wife, Tanaquil, kept the king's death secret for a time, and thereby contrived to secure the succession to her son-in-law.

Servius Tullius, who reigned from B.C. 578 to 534, is described, like his father-in-law, as a foreigner. His origin, however, is uncertain, and very wonderful stories are related of his early life. After he had ascended the throne, he is said to have undertaken a successful war against Veii, or, as some state, against all Etruria. But the glory of his reign did not consist in military undertakings, but in the fact that he gave to the Roman people a new constitution, which, with some changes, was retained by the Romans as long as they enjoyed any constitution at all.

Hitherto the patricians alone had formed the sovereign people (*populus Romanus*), while the plebeians had had to perform all the duties of citizens, without enjoying the rights of citizens. Servius Tullius first organised the whole body of the plebeians, by dividing them into thirty local divisions, called tribes, four of which belonged to the city, and the remaining twenty-six to the country around it. Each tribe received its own magistrate, called *tribunus*, and the thirty tribes obtained the right to meet and discuss their own affairs. These meetings were called *comitia tributa*, to distinguish them from those of the patricians, called *comitia curiata*. A far more important reform was that he framed a constitution, by which a man's rights and duties were determined, not as hitherto, by birth alone, but by the amount of property he possessed. For this purpose he instituted a census, and according to it divided the whole people, both patricians and plebeians, into five property classes, the first of which possessed at least 100,000 asses, and the fifth at least 12,500. Those who had less than this minimum constituted the large class of what were called proletarians or *capite censi*, who did not belong to any class. Each class had assigned to it a number of votes or centuries (*centuriæ*). The first class had eighty, the second, third, and fourth twenty each, the fifth thirty, while the proletarians had only one, making altogether 171 centuries or votes. In addition to these the eighteen centuries of equites had eighteen votes, and carpenters and musicians had each two, so that the whole number of votes amounted to 193. The distribution of votes therefore was such, that when the first class and the eighteen centuries of equites agreed among themselves, a majority was obtained, and there was no need for the other classes to vote. All political power was thus vested in the wealthiest classes, so that for the moment the king's reform probably did not cause any violent change, except that the plebeians obtained the right to take part in the great national assembly of the centuries (*comitia centuriata*), which at the same time represented the whole Roman people as an army, inasmuch as the class to which a man belonged determined the duties he had to perform as a soldier. To this new assembly were transferred all the more important rights which had previously belonged exclusively to the patrician *comitia curiata*.

Instead of continuing the war against the Latins, he managed to induce them to acknowledge the supremacy of Rome by peaceful means. He induced them, and apparently the Sabines also, to found a sanctuary to Diana on the Aventine. Lastly, he carried out the design of his predecessor, to surround the city with a wall, in which he included two more hills, the Viminal and Esquiline. By these things, and especially by his political reforms, Servius Tullius drew upon himself the hatred of the patricians, who, headed by Tarquinius, his own son-in-law, created a revolution, in which the aged king was murdered, and Tarquinius ascended the throne.

The account of this revolution runs as follows : In order to propitiate the sons of his predecessor, and to secure to them the succession, Servius had given his two daughters in marriage to the two sons of Tarquinius Priscus, Lucius and Aruns. The former, though capable of criminal actions, was not naturally disposed to crime, but he was married to a gentle and unambitious woman ; while the wife of his gentle brother Aruns, called Tullia, was still more passionate and ambitious than her brother-in-law. Tullia, vexed at the long life of her father, and at the indifference of her husband, who seemed willing to leave the succession to his more ambitious brother, planned the destruction of those who seemed to stand in her husband's way to the throne. A secret understanding was easily come to between her and Lucius, who was induced to kill his wife, while she murdered her husband. This design being accomplished, she and Lucius became united in marriage. Lucius, goaded on by his unscrupulous wife, formed a conspiracy with discontented patricians, and it was resolved to destroy the aged king. Tarquinius then summoned a meeting of the senate, and, adorned with the ensigns of royalty and accompanied by a band of armed followers, he entered the senate, delivered a wild speech against Servius Tullius, and tried to establish his legal claim to the throne. The king, when informed of these proceedings, hastened to the senate, intending to put a stop to such revolutionary proceedings. But Lucius

Tarquinius seized the feeble and defenceless old man, and hurled him down the steps of the senate house. When the old man tried to escape by flight, armed men were sent after him, who slew him, and left him a corpse in the street, covered with blood. Meanwhile Tullia also had driven to the senate, to receive the first news of her husband's success, and to congratulate him. This unnatural conduct was too much even for Lucius Tarquinius, who ordered her to return home. On her way, the chariot passed through the street in which her father's body was lying. The mules, on approaching it, reared, and the driver stopped; but Tullia ordered him to drive on, and the chariot passed over her father's body, the blood of which stained the garment of the unnatural daughter. The street in which this had happened was ever after called the accursed street (*Vicus Sceleratus*).

Lucius Tarquinius now reigned in a manner worthy of the means by which he had usurped the throne, that is, he acted as a tyrant, whence he has obtained the surname of *Superbus*, which signifies the haughty or the insolent. During his reign, which lasted from B.C. 534 to 510, he neither consulted the senate nor the people, but followed his own personal inclinations in everything. The reforms of Servius Tullius were abolished, and the labours of that king seemed to have been spent in vain. The acts of cruelty and oppression ascribed to him are almost incredible; but however this may be, it cannot be denied that he must have been a man of great military ability, for he extended his kingdom more than any of his predecessors, and adorned the city with great and useful architectural works. He compelled the Latin towns to conclude a treaty with him, in which Rome was recognised as the head of all the Latins. He conquered Suessa Pometia, a wealthy town of the Volscians, and strengthened the power of Rome by the establishment of the colonies of Signia and Circeii, whereby the conquered people were kept in subjection. But notwithstanding these military achievements, his unpopularity was daily increasing, both with the senators and with

the people; many of the former were put to death or
sent into exile, while the people were groaning under
their heavy taxes, and the task-work imposed upon them
in the construction of public buildings. The king, it is
said, was further harassed by dreams and awful prodigies.
Uneasy at all these symptoms of the discontent of his
subjects, and the anger of the gods, he sent two of his
sons, Titus and Aruns, to consult the oracle of Delphi.
To amuse them on their journey, he sent with them a
cousin, *Lucius Junius Brutus*, who had assumed the
character of an idiot, in order to escape the danger of
being put to death. When the princes had executed
their father's orders at Delphi, they also consulted the
god about themselves; and the answer was, that he should
be king of Rome who should be the first to kiss his
mother. The two brothers agreed to kiss their mother
at the same time, so that they might rule in common;
but on their landing in Italy, Brutus, as if falling by
accident, without being observed, kissed the earth, the
mother of all.

During the latter part of his reign, Tarquinius was
involved in a war with Ardea, a fortified town of the
Rutulians, who had probably refused to acknowledge the
supremacy of Rome. The town accordingly was besieged,
but with little success; and one day, while the king's
sons and their cousin, Tarquinius Collatinus, were feast-
ing in their tents and discussing the virtues of their
wives, it was arranged that the three should go home
unexpectedly by night, to see how the princesses were
spending their time. The wives of the two brothers
were found at Rome, revelling at a luxurious banquet;
but when they came to Collatia, they found *Lucretia*,
the wife of Tarquinius Collatinus, engaged in domestic
occupations with her maid-servants. She accordingly
was acknowledged to be the best of the three; but in
her humble occupation she appeared so lovely and beautiful, that a few days later Sextus Tarquinius, one of the
princes, returned to Collatia, where, as a kinsman, he
was hospitably received. But in the dead of night he

entered her chamber, and threatened to expose her name to everlasting shame, if she refused to gratify his lust. By intimidation he gained his end. But on the following morning Lucretia sent for her father and husband, who came accompanied by Publius Valerius and Lucius Junius Brutus. To these four men Lucretia revealed the crime committed upon her, and having called upon them to avenge the wrong, plunged a dagger into her own breast. Brutus now throwing off the mask of idiotcy, and drawing the dagger from the wound, vowed destruction to the royal house of the Tarquins. The three others took the same oath, and the people of Collatia having been informed of what had happened, at once took up arms. The conspirators then hastened to Rome, summoned an assembly of the people, where it was unanimously decreed to depose and banish the whole royal family. Brutus, who is said to have held the office of commander of the horse (*tribunus celerum*), then set out for Ardea to gain over the army. The king, as soon as he heard the news, hastened to Rome, in the hope of being able to quell the insurrection, but found the gates closed against him. Meanwhile the army also followed the summons of Brutus; and the king, with his queen and two of his sons, took refuge at Cære in Etruria. His son Sextus went to Gabii, where soon after he was slain on account of an act of treachery he had previously committed against that town.

Such is the traditional story of a revolution which for ever put an end to the kingly government. How much of it may be true cannot possibly be ascertained; but there can be no doubt that Tarquinius Superbus was the last king of Rome, and that his reign had been very despotic, though tradition may have much exaggerated his misdeeds. Whether, however, the revolution was accomplished in the quick and quiet manner described in the legend, is more than doubtful.

We have seen that the Roman kings were raised to the throne by election, and it is only under the later kings that we hear of sons claiming to succeed their fathers. The time during which the seven kings are said to have reigned is unusually long; and there is good reason for believing that the whole kingly period was made up artificially, for every one of the kings is represented as having founded one or other of the great institutions of the kingdom; nay, it is even doubtful whether Rome had only seven kings. But certain it is, that the king was elected from among the patricians, at first alternately from the Ramnes and the Sabines; that he was the chief commander of the armies, the supreme judge, and the high priest of the nation. His power, however, was not absolute, for on all important matters he had to consult the senate. The number of senators being three hundred, seems to suggest that they were chosen by the king to represent the three patrician tribes. The king's power was further limited by the assembly of the old citizens or patricians (*comitia curiata*), until, by the reforms of Servius Tullius, the great national assembly (*comitia centuriata*) stepped into its place. All matters that were laid before the assembly, such as questions about peace and war, the election of magistrates, and proposals of new laws, were first considered by the senate, and when sanctioned by that body, were brought before the assembly, which might either adopt or reject them.

As to the civilisation of the Romans during the regal period, we have seen that they had a regularly organised form of government, that they dwelt in fortified towns, had regular armies, and lived chiefly by agriculture and the breeding of cattle. During the later period they constructed great architectural works, such as the great Temple of Jupiter on the Capitol, which was completed by Tarquinius Superbus; and the great sewers, parts of which still exist in a perfect state of preservation. The religion of the Romans also seems to have undergone considerable changes during the reign of the Tarquins, for it is in the reign of the last of them that we hear of the gods being represented in human forms. The legendary history further reveals to us the mode of life of those early Romans, who do not seem to have been very far behind in their social life from that of our own ancestors. The art of writing, with which the Romans became acquainted through the Greeks settled in southern Italy, appears to have been introduced in the time of the first Tarquin, but was certainly not employed for literary purposes. Money was first coined by Servius Tullius; it consisted of brass marked with the figure of some domestic animal, whence the Latin name for money is *pecunia* (from *pecus*, cattle).

JUNIUS BRUTUS

THE BATTERING-RAM.

CHAPTER II.

FROM THE ESTABLISHMENT OF THE REPUBLIC TO THE LEGISLATION OF THE DECEMVIRS.

B.C. 509 TO B.C. 451.

AFTER the expulsion of Tarquinius, in B.C. 509, the people assembled in the comitia centuriata formally abolished the kingly power for ever, restored the constitution of Servius Tullius, and elected two magistrates from among the patricians, who, under the title of *prætors*, afterwards called *consuls*, were to conduct the government for one year. The first prætors or consuls were *Lucius Junius Brutus* and *Tarquinius Collatinus*, who had the same power and the same outward distinctions as the kings, except that the priestly functions of the king were transferred to a dignitary styled *rex sacrorum* or *rex sacrificulus*, and that the administration of the treasury was assigned to two officers called *quæstores ærarii*. The senate and the comitia centuriata, of course, retained the powers assigned to them by the Servian constitution. The power of the patricians, instead of being diminished by the establishment of a republic, was in reality somewhat increased, inasmuch as two of their body might every year be raised to the highest magistracy. The plebeians, on the other hand, were probably in a worse condition than they had been under the kings, as the latter would naturally favour the plebeians in order to have in them a support against the arrogant and ambitious patricians; they were still excluded from all public offices, from the right of contracting legal marriages with the patricians, and other privileges reserved for the ruling citizens. In the great national assembly they appeared indeed on a footing of equality with the patricians; but the latter, by the overwhelming number of their votes, were enabled to carry every measure, so that the power of the plebeians was in reality only nominal. The administration of the laws, moreover, was still entirely in the hands of the patricians. Under such circumstances, a conflict between the two estates, sooner or later, was unavoidable.

The young republic, in order to secure its existence, had to struggle against domestic as well as foreign enemies, by whose assistance Tarquinius hoped to effect his restoration. In the very first year, a conspiracy was formed among a number of young patricians for the purpose of restoring the exiled monarch; they were joined even by the sons of Brutus. When it was found out, the guilty were put to death, and Brutus, with a sternness peculiarly characteristic of a Roman, ordered his own sons to be executed. But a greater danger came from Etruria, where Tarquinius had asked and obtained the assistance of *Porsenna*, lars or king of Clusium. The Etruscans are said to have marched against Rome and to have pitched their camp on Mount Janiculum, on the right bank of the Tiber. The accounts of this war represent the valour and daring of the Romans in the most brilliant colours, though as we shall see hereafter, the whole has been much embellished and exaggerated by oral tradition. On one occasion, it is said, the Romans crossed the Tiber with the intention of driving the enemy from his stronghold, but were repulsed and returned to the city; and the enemy would have pursued them across the river, had not *Horatius Cocles*, a bold and powerful Roman, who was guarding the wooden bridge with two comrades, kept the whole hostile army at bay, while his countrymen were busily engaged in breaking down the bridge. He is even said to have dismissed his two comrades and alone to have resisted the whole army until the bridge was demolished. He then threw himself into the river, and safely swam across, amid showers of darts from the Etruscans. He was afterwards rewarded by his countrymen with a statue in the Comitium, the place of assembly of the patricians, and with as much land as he could plough round in a day. A similar story of daring is related about one *Mucius Scævola.* As during the protracted siege Rome was beginning to suffer from famine, young Scævola, with the consent of the senate, undertook to deliver his country from the enemy by murdering Porsenna. He contrived to find his way to the tent of the Etruscan chief, but by a mistake slew the king's scribe instead of the king himself. He was accordingly seized at once, and as the king tried by threats to extort from him a full confession of his object, Scævola thrust his right hand into the fire which was burning upon an altar, to show that he dreaded neither torture nor death. The king, full of admiration of the young man's daring, dismissed him, but was told that 300 other Roman youths had sworn to take the king's life. The king, frightened at this, negotiated a peace with the Romans, only demanding that the territory taken from Veii should be restored, whereupon he withdrew with his army.

However delightful such stories are which the vanity of the Romans in after-times invented to embellish the first struggles of their republic, we know upon good authority that Porsenna for a time was master of Rome, and consented to depart only on receiving hostages and one-third of the Roman territory—that is, ten out of the thirty local tribes. The unhistorical character of the stories is further evident from the fact that the exiled Tarquinius is never once mentioned during the war with Porsenna, who himself likewise entirely disappears after the war.

Some other tribes also, such as the Sabines and Auruncans, are said to have waged war against Rome, but unsuccessfully. A more formidable war broke out in B.C. 501 with the Latins, whom Tarquinius had stirred up against the Romans through the influence of some of his Latin kinsmen. All the Latin towns rose against Rome, and the war was protracted for several years. At last, in B.C. 498, the Romans thinking it safer to entrust the conduct of the war to a single commander instead of the two consuls, appointed Titus Larcius dictator with full power. This measure is said to have kept the enemies in awe, but still the war was continued for two years longer, until in B.C. 496 it was brought to an end by the famous battle on the shores of Lake Regillus. In it the Romans were victorious, and it was currently said that the gods Castor and Pollux had been seen fighting on their side. The account of this battle, which may be said to form the close of the legendary period of Roman history, is altogether unworthy of belief, for, three years later, the Latins concluded a treaty with the Roman consul *Spurius Cassius* in which they were placed on a footing of perfect equality with Rome, without any further war being mentioned to account for this favour. King Tarquinius himself is said to have been wounded in the battle, and to have withdrawn to Aristodemus, the tyrant of Cumæ, where he died in the following year, B.C. 495.

As long as Rome had to contend against foreign enemies, the patricians managed to keep the plebeians, who formed the main strength of the Roman armies, in good humour; but no sooner had the dangers disappeared, than they began to abuse their privileged position against the plebeians, whom they treated as their subjects. We have already seen that they were conquered Latins who, though free, did not possess the franchise, but were obliged to pay tribute to the republic and serve in the armies without pay. It often happened that, when they were engaged against foreign enemies, their fields (for they were mostly small landed proprietors), if not ravaged or taken by the enemy, were at any rate neglected, so that at harvest time there was nothing to reap. The result of this was, that in their distress they had often to borrow money of their wealthy neighbours, generally patricians, at the exorbitant rate of interest of from ten to twelve per cent.; and the severity of the Roman law entitled the creditor, if the debtor did not repay the borrowed money at the stipulated time, to seize his person and treat him as if he were his slave. From such misery the patricians were exempted, inasmuch as their estates were cultivated by their clients, who did not serve in war. Such a state of things naturally became more and more unbearable, and as the patricians had the law on their side, the plebeians in B.C. 495, rose in open rebellion and withdrew to a hill a few miles distant from Rome, resolved not to return until their grievances should be redressed. Several attempts were made to pacify them, but with no result, until Menenius Agrippa, a messenger of the senate, prevailed upon them, by the well-known fable of the belly and the members, to abandon their design, and promised that their grievances should be remedied. A compact was then concluded between the patricians and plebeians, that all who had lost their freedom through debt should be set free, and that five tribunes of the plebs should be appointed, whose duty it was to be to protect the plebeians against any abuse of the authority of a patrician magistrate, and whose persons were to be sacred and inviolate. At the same time two plebeian ædiles were appointed, whose business it was to superintend the public buildings and to exercise a sort of control over merchants and usurers. When this solemn compact was concluded, the plebeians quitted the hill, which was ever after called the Sacred Mount, and returned to Rome.

Such was the beginning of the long protracted struggle between the two orders, throughout which the patricians acted more or less the part of an exclusive aristocracy, while the plebeians represented what we may call the great body of the people. The tenacity and selfishness with which the former clung to their rights and privileges, and the indomitable perseverance of the latter to obtain the full civic franchise, constitute for some centuries the most interesting portion in the development of the Roman state. Had the patricians succeeded, Rome would have become a rigid oligarchy, and would never have played any important part in the world's history. It was owing to the persevering resistance of the plebeians that Rome gradually developed into a mighty state, and in the end became the mistress of the ancient world.

During the secession of the plebs, agriculture had of course been almost entirely neglected, and Rome was beginning to suffer from famine. When at length ships laden with corn arrived from Sicily, the insolent patrician *Marcius Coriolanus* proposed that none of it should be given to the plebeians unless they renounced all the advantages gained by the compact of the Sacred Mount. At this the plebeians were so exasperated that their tribunes brought an action against him, in which he was outlawed. He accordingly, in B.C. 491, took refuge as an exile among the Volscians, whom he instigated to wage war against Rome, promising that he would act as their guide and leader. Under his command the Volscians and Æquians advanced within a few miles of Rome, and nothing could induce him to abandon his unpatriotic undertaking, until he was prevailed upon by the tears and entreaties of his wife and mother. Coriolanus is said to have died soon after, overwhelmed with grief and shame; but the Volscians retained possession of some important Latin towns they had taken.

In the year B.C. 486, the same *Spurius Cassius* who had concluded the alliance with the Latins, brought about another on equal terms with the Hernicans, so that now the Romans, Latins, and Hernicans formed a strong confederacy against any foreign enemies. About the same time the first attempt was made to legislate about the public or domain land (*ager publicus*). These lands having been acquired by conquest, were very extensive, and belonged not to any individual, but to the state, that is, to the populus or patricians, who took possession of it on condition of their paying a nominal rent to the treasury. They knew, of course, that the state might reclaim such lands at any time, but they nevertheless gradually came to regard them as their private property, and had them cultivated by their clients and slaves. Spurius Cassius, in his third consulship, B.C. 486, was the first Roman who proposed and carried an agrarian law, enacting that a certain portion of the public land should be assigned to those plebeians who did not possess any landed property. His noble efforts to prevent the growth of pauperism, and to transform a number of poor plebeians into industrious husbandmen, were ill requited, for when he laid down his consulship he was accused by his fellow patricians of high treason, condemned, and beheaded. The house in which he had lived was razed to the ground, and its site declared accursed ground. The patricians scrupled at nothing to prevent the law, though passed in due form, being carried into effect. Many years later, B.C. 473, the tribune *Genucius* arraigned the consuls for not allowing the law to be carried out; but on the morning before the day of the trial he was found murdered in his own house. Such acts of violence for a time intimidated the plebeians and their friends, but they still persevered, and, as we shall see, in the end compelled the patricians to yield.

The internal feuds between the two orders had the effect of weakening the power of Rome so much, that the Etruscans and Æquians were enabled to make themselves masters of several of the towns subject to Rome. The war against the Etruscans especially went on for a long time without any advantage to the Romans. There was at the time a Roman clan, called the Fabia gens, consisting of 306 men, who before this time had been proud and haughty champions of their order against the plebeians, but afterwards are said to have changed their minds and to have sided with the plebeians, which brought upon them the hatred of their fellow patricians. They now proposed to the senate to carry on the long protracted war against the Etruscan town of Veii at their own expense. The request was granted, and the whole clan proceeding against the enemy, ravaged the country, and were successful in many an enterprise. But in the end they were drawn into an ambuscade, and the whole clan was surrounded and cut to pieces, in B.C. 477, on the banks of the river Cremera. Only one young member of the clan who had remained behind at Rome survived, and became the ancestor of the Fabii whom we meet with in the subsequent history of Rome. This story of the Fabii seems to be only a popular legend, though it probably had some historical foundation, for it must be remembered that, although the battle of Lake Regillus may be regarded as concluding the mythical or legendary period, many of the subsequent events are still far from being well authenticated, the Romans themselves in their vanity having exaggerated and embellished many of the occurrences of their early history.

While Rome was thus engaged against the Etruscans, the Æquians and Volscians also continued their inroads into the Roman territory. The former, it is said, had concluded a peace with Rome; but their commander, Gracchus Cloelius, nevertheless continued hostilities from Mount Algidus. At last, the Roman consul Minucius, after having been defeated, was besieged in his own camp. Five horsemen who had escaped before the camp was surrounded, brought the sad news to Rome; and the senate at once appointed *Quinctius Cincinnatus* dictator, B.C. 458. The news of his elevation was brought to him on his farm, which he cultivated with his own hands. He appointed Tarquitius his master of the horse, and in three days he succeeded in enlisting a numerous army, with which he marched to Mount Algidus. The Romans having received a signal that succour had arrived, broke through the surrounding enemy, and a desperate battle commenced, in which the Æquians, seeing no means of escape, implored Cincinnatus to spare them. The Æquian commander and the leading officers were put in chains, while the rest of the army had to lay down their arms and pass under the yoke, a sign of humiliation to which the Romans usually subjected a defeated foe. The town of Corbio and the camp of the enemy fell into the hands of the Romans. Cincinnatus then returned to Rome in triumph, and was rewarded with a golden crown. He had held the dictatorship for no more than sixteen days, and laying down his office, he returned to his farm. This story also seems to be only a popular legend embodying the simple fact that Minucius was saved by succour being sent to him from Rome. The Æquians, however, continued the war with varying success until B.C. 446, when the great battle of Corbio weakened them so much that for a time they were obliged to remain quiet.

There existed as yet at Rome no code of written laws. The making as well as the administration of the laws based upon ancient usage, was altogether in the hands of the patricians, who were often guilty of acts of flagrant injustice. The plebeians, beginning to feel their power more and more, demanded that a code of laws should be drawn up, which might give them a knowledge of the laws and of the forms of procedure. The patricians, unwilling to give up any of their privileges, violently opposed the demand; but in B.C. 471, the tribune, *Publilius Volero*, in spite of the most determined opposition, carried several laws enacting that the plebeian magistrates should be elected in the comitia tributa, and that these comitia should have the power to pass resolutions upon matters affecting the interests of the whole state. These measures created the greatest excitement, and the exasperation between the patricians and plebeians produced a complete division among the Roman citizens. At the same time, the city was visited by an epidemic which carried off large numbers of all ranks. By these circumstances Rome was so much weakened, that the Æquians and Volscians carried their predatory inroads up to the very gates of Rome.

The first formal demand for a written code of laws was made in B.C. 462 by the tribune *Terentillus Arsa*. The scheme was violently opposed by the patricians, but to no purpose, for similar demands continued to be repeated, as the plebeians were determined to gain their point. In B.C. 457, a law was passed increasing the number of tribunes from five to ten, for it seems to have been found that five were not sufficient to afford protection to the

HISTORY OF ROME.

plebeians in all cases. In B.C. 454, the bill of Terentillus Arsa was brought forward again, and it was at last resolved that the law should be revised, and that three senators should be sent to Athens to study the laws and constitution of that and other Greek states, and to report on such laws and institutions as might seem applicable to Rome.

CORIOLANUS, HIS WIFE, AND MOTHER.

A BRONZE COIN.

CHAPTER III.

FROM THE DECEMVIRAL LEGISLATION TO THE FINAL SUBJUGATION OF LATIUM.

B.C. 451 TO B.C. 338.

WHEN the three ambassadors returned from Greece and had made their report, it was resolved to appoint a commission of ten patricians (*decemviri*) to draw up a code of laws, that they should have full power to act in all matters according to their own discretion, and that the powers of all other magistrates should be suspended while the decemvirs were engaged on their work. The decemvirs entered upon their task in B.C. 451, and performed their duties honestly and satisfactorily; but as at the end of the first year their work was still incomplete, they were permitted to continue in office for another year. The decemvirs now began to act in the most arbitrary and cruel manner against every one who ventured to express an opinion upon their doings; nay, an aged and brave plebeian, whose opposition they feared, and who happened to be serving in the army, was drawn into a snare and murdered at the instigation of the decemvirs.

At the end of the second year, the decemvirs, although their task was completed, and the laws were engraved upon twelve tables, still persisted in retaining their office, and might perhaps have succeeded in establishing a patrician oligarchy, had not the haughty and insolent *Appius Claudius*, the most influential among them, by a glaring act of injustice, called forth a general rising of the people against them. Claudius had conceived a desire to obtain possession of the beautiful Virginia, the daughter of the plebeian Virginius. In order to gain his object, he persuaded one of his clients to declare the maiden to be a runaway slave of his own, and to claim her as his property before Claudius himself. A large concourse of people assembled, and Claudius did not scruple to declare that Virginia belonged to his client. But her father, having obtained permission to take her aside for a few moments for the purpose of taking leave, plunged a knife into her heart to save her from dishonour.

The infamous act of Claudius created the greatest excitement in the city. The authority of the decemvirs was at once set at defiance; and the army, which happened to be engaged against the Sabines, on hearing what had happened, proceeded to Mount Aventine, where they took up a strong position; and the plebeians, with their wives and children, emigrated to the Sacred Mount, resolved to leave Rome and seek a new home elsewhere. Valerius and Horatius, the two most popular among the patricians, were despatched by the senate to treat with the plebeians, and come to an understanding with them on the best terms they could. The plebeians demanded the deposition of the decemvirs, and for themselves a complete amnesty, and the right of appeal against any patrician magistrate. These demands being granted and sanctioned by the senate, the plebeians returned to the city. Appius Claudius was thrown into prison, where he committed suicide; one of his colleagues died in the same manner, and the remaining eight went into exile.

But the new laws enacted by the decemvirs and engraved upon twelve tables, remained in force, and were set up in public. They mostly referred to the civil and criminal law, and ever after formed the basis of the whole

of the Roman law. The only constitutional change which
they seem to have introduced was that henceforth the
patricians should become members of the local plebeian
tribes. But no great power could be exercised by the
patricians in the assembly of the tribes, as the tribes
could not yet influence the making of new laws. The
only gain for the plebeians was that the laws had become
fixed, so that the commonalty was no longer exposed to
the arbitrary proceedings of the patricians. In all other
respects their condition remained the same as before, for
they were still excluded from the highest offices of the
state, as well as from participating in the public land,
nor could a plebeian contract a legal marriage with a
patrician.

Although the patricians, by recent experience, ought
to have learned that their selfishness and avarice could
lead only to most unfortunate results, they still continued
to annoy and oppress the plebeians in every way; and
although the more daring among the latter sometimes
felt inclined to take vengeance into their own hands, the
great body of the plebeians were moderate but firm, and
showed a determination, in the course of time, to gain
for themselves perfect equality with the patricians.

In the year B.C. 445, the tribune *Canuleius* brought
forward a bill demanding for the plebeians the right of
contracting legal marriages (*connubium*) with patricians;
and the bill was passed in spite of the fiercest opposition.
In another bill he proposed that it should be left optional
to the people to elect one of the two consuls from among
the plebeians. The latter of these bills gave rise to many
long and violent discussions; but in the end it was agreed
that instead of consuls, *military tribunes with consular
power* should be elected and taken indiscriminately from
the plebeians as well as from the patricians. The senate,
however, reserved to itself the power of determining
whether in any given year the highest authority should
be entrusted to consuls as before, or to military tribunes.
By this means the consulship was reserved for the patricians, who in many cases also contrived to keep the mili-

tary tribuneship within their own order. The patricians, however, seem to have foreseen that sooner or later the plebeians would gain their end; and in order that they might never enjoy the full powers of the consulship, two censors were appointed, in B.C. 443, whose functions had previously been connected with the consulship. This new office was to be open to patricians only, and was filled up every five years (*lustrum*), though the censors had to perform their duties within the space of eighteen months. Their chief functions were to draw up lists of all Roman citizens, in which they were classed according to their rank and property. They had further to collect the rent for the domain land, to give in contract the building of temples and the making of roads and bridges; they further exercised a severe control over the morals of the citizens, and were empowered to punish offences against morality by depriving the offenders of their civil rights, or of their rank and station in society. The verdict of a censor, however, was not permanent, but might be reversed by his successor.

The advantages gained by the plebeians through recent legislation somewhat softened the animosity between the two orders of citizens; but still the patricians never neglected an opportunity of annoying and humbling the plebeians. Thus, when in B.C. 440 Rome was visited by a famine, and when all endeavours to mitigate the evil were of no avail, a wealthy plebeian, *Spurius Mælius*, purchased large quantities of grain and sold it at a moderate price to the famishing people, in consequence of which he acquired great influence. His popularity alarmed the patricians, and fearing treacherous plots and conspiracies, they charged him with the crime of endeavouring to make himself king of Rome. The aged Quinctius Cincinnatus being appointed dictator, in B.C. 439 summoned Mælius before his tribunal, and as Mælius refused to appear, he was slain in broad daylight by Servilius Ahala, the dictator's master of the horse.

During these internal agitations the Roman armies fought many successful battles against their enemies; and

Rome, strengthened by the alliance with the Latins and Hernicans, gained repeated victories over the Volscians and Æquians. The town of Fidenæ, an ancient Roman colony, was destroyed in B.C. 426, because it had committed many outrages against Rome. During its last struggle it had been supported by the Etruscan city of Veii. In consequence of this, Veii became involved in a long and desperate war with Rome, which had to direct all its forces against this enemy. The war is said to have lasted ten years, and to have been ultimately, in B.C. 396, brought to an end by *Camillus.* The story of the siege and capture of Veii is indeed mixed up with many fables, but it is pretty certain that most of its inhabitants were destroyed and the rest sold as slaves. During this protracted war it became evident that it was most injurious and inconvenient for the men to remain so long absent from home, and the senate of its own accord decreed that in future the soldiers should receive pay from the public treasury, for until then they had been obliged to equip and maintain themselves. Camillus, the conqueror of Veii, celebrated a magnificent triumph; but as he was believed to have appropriated to himself more than his legitimate share in the booty, and refused to consent to the territory of Veii being distributed among the plebeians, he became extremely unpopular, and in B.C. 391 he was publicly accused of having secreted a portion of the spoil taken at Veii. In order to escape condemnation he went into voluntary exile, declaring when he left Rome that the time would soon come when his help would be needed. And he was not wrong, for Rome was on the eve of coming in conflict with an enemy more formidable than any she had yet encountered.

Swarms of Gauls are said to have crossed the Alps as early as the reign of Tarquinius Priscus, and to have driven those Etruscans who until then had occupied the plains of Lombardy, across the Apennines into the country which ever after bore their name. For a time the Apennines formed the barrier between them and the Etruscans; but in B.C. 390 large bodies of Gauls crossed the mountains, and, under the command of a chief called *Brennus*, laid siege to the Etruscan town of Clusium. Its inhabitants, looking round for assistance, applied to the Romans, who at first only sent ambassadors to the Gauls to remonstrate with them; but as the barbarians paid no attention to them, the ambassadors took part in a battle which ensued, and slew one of the Gallic chiefs. The Gauls complained of this violation of the law of nations, and demanded the surrender of the offenders; and as this was haughtily refused, they at once gave up the siege of Clusium, and marched southward towards Rome. They met a Roman army on the banks of the little river *Allia*, about eleven miles from Rome, and so completely defeated it, that only a few survived the day. They then advanced to Rome, which was in a defenceless state, and easily fell into the hands of the invaders. The city was set on fire, and eighty senators, resolved to devote themselves as a propitiatory sacrifice to the gods, sat down in their curule chairs in the Forum, and were ruthlessly massacred. The Capitol alone, to which many of the most valuable treasures had been carried, was defended by a small garrison under the command of *Manlius Capitolinus*. The Gauls, elated with their recent victory, abandoned themselves to every kind of excess, in consequence of which many perished during the protracted siege of the Capitol, which lasted for seven months. Tradition says that Brennus, induced by these calamities, entered into negotiation with the Romans, and accepted a thousand pounds of gold on condition that he should quit the territory of Rome, but that he insolently increased the amount of gold by throwing his sword into the scale containing the weights. At this moment Camillus, who had been recalled from his exile, arrived with a fresh army at the gates of Rome, where he utterly annihilated the enemy, and recovered all the booty which they had intended to carry off. This story of the sacking and burning of Rome by the Gauls is indeed an historical fact, but the account of the manner in which the Romans got rid of the enemy is a mere fiction invented by Roman vanity, for it is now a well-known fact that the Gauls departed from Rome with their booty unmolested, because their own country beyond the Apennines had in the meantime been invaded by other swarms of Gauls descending from the Alps.

When the Gauls left Rome a heap of blackened ruins, the people were not inclined to restore their habitations, and proposed to emigrate and take possession of the deserted city of Veii. The patricians, however, clinging to their ancient homes, with great difficulty prevailed upon the people to abandon their design, but allowed them to demolish the houses still standing at Veii, and use the materials in rebuilding their own homes at Rome. Rome was thus hastily restored, and as little attention could be paid to beauty and order, the streets ever after were narrow, crooked, and irregular. The sufferings of the people must have been very severe in consequence of the ravages and devastations of the Gauls, and many had fallen into great poverty; but the patricians applied the law of debt, which had not been altered in the Twelve Tables, with the utmost rigour, and many poor plebeians were pining away in the dungeons of the patricians. Their condition at last excited the sympathy of the brave Manlius Capitolinus, who proposed a general reduction of the debts and a distribution of the public land among the impoverished people. This proposal exasperated his brother patricians to such a degree that they brought against him the futile charge of aiming at kingly power, and procured his condemnation. The man who had saved the Capitol was accordingly thrown down the Tarpeian Rock, his house was razed to the ground, and his name treated as that of an accursed person. These disgraceful proceedings took place in the year B.C. 384.

But these were not the only misfortunes resulting from the Gallic invasion, for during the humiliation of Rome the Hernicans and many Latin towns renounced their alliance with her, and the Volscians, Æquians, and Etruscans resumed their hostilities. The last three of these nations were defeated one after another by Camillus, the greatest general of the period, and Sutrium and Nepete in Etruria were made Roman colonies to keep the country in subjection. Some of the Latin towns also were reduced to submission, and Rome was rapidly recovering from the evils of the late invasion. In order to pacify the more clamorous among the poor, the senate in B.C. 383, had assigned the Pomptine district to the poor plebeians. But the murder of Manlius, their champion, roused the plebeians to more vigorous resistance to their oppressors. At last, in B.C. 376, *Licinius Stolo* and *Lucius Sextius*, two bold and energetic tribunes, undertook to introduce such reforms as might still save Rome from falling into a state of anarchy. They brought forward three bills: (1.) that henceforth two consuls should be elected annually, as of old, but that one of them should always be a plebeian; (2.) that no one should be allowed to occupy more than five hundred jugera (acres) of the public land, that the surplus should be taken from the former occupants and given to the plebeians as their full property; and (3.) that the interest already paid upon debts should be deducted from the principal, and that the remainder should be paid off by three yearly instalments. For a period of nearly ten years the patricians did everything to prevent these bills from becoming law; but all their contrivances to thwart them, and even the elevation of Camillus to the dictatorship, were of no avail against the firmness and perseverance of the tribunes; for the tribunes, who had by this time acquired much greater power than was entrusted to them at their first appointment, continued to prevent the election of magistrates and the levies for the armies by their *veto*, whereby they could stop any public act of a magistrate. At length, in B.C. 367, after a long period of strife and anarchy, the patricians felt themselves compelled to give way: the bills of the tribunes became law, and the year after Lucius Sextius was elected the first plebeian consul. But being obliged to give up the consulship, the patricians again contrived to strip it of one of its main functions, that is, the jurisdiction in civil cases, which was now assigned to a special officer called *Prætor*, who was to be chosen exclusively from among the patricians. But such reservations and precautions were of little use, for ten years later, B.C. 356, a plebeian was appointed dictator; in B.C. 351 a plebeian was made censor; in B.C. 337 a plebeian obtained the prætorship; and in B.C. 300 the priestly offices of pontifex and augur were thrown open to the plebeians. By these successive reforms the two orders were gradually placed on a footing of equality; and Rome, internally united and strong, was enabled to enter upon the grand career assigned to it by Providence.

The reconciliation effected between the two orders had many opportunities of showing its good results, for very soon after, Rome had to contend not only against swarms of Gauls who still overran and ravaged Italy, but against the most powerful nation in Central Italy. It was in the course of these Gallic wars that Caius Marcius was the first plebeian dictator, B.C. 356, and that *Manlius Torquatus* and *Valerius Corvus* are said to have distinguished themselves by deeds of valour that have rendered their names immortal. In B.C. 358, it is said, the Gauls had pitched their camp on the banks of the Allia, and a Gaul of gigantic stature, stepping on the bridge separating the two armies, challenged any Roman to fight him. Titus Manlius, a young Roman, with the consul's permission, accepted the challenge, and, lightly armed, he advanced against the Gallic giant, and pressed on him so closely that the barbarian was unable to use his arms against him. Manlius pierced him with his sword through the side and belly, and when the enemy lay prostrate on the ground, Manlius stripped him of his gold chain (*torques*) and put it round his own neck. From this circumstance he received the surname of Torquatus. Eight years later, when another swarm of Gauls appeared in the very neighbourhood of Rome, a powerful barbarian, according to the usual custom of his nation, challenged the bravest of the Romans to a single combat. Marcus Valerius, a young tribune of the soldiers, came forward, and when the combat began, a raven (*corvus*) which had settled upon the helmet of Valerius, at every onset flew into the face of the Gaul, who, being thus unable to see, was slain by the young Roman. The latter, from this wonderful ally, received the surname of Corvus.

The success of the Romans in these Gallic wars, as already observed, was owing to some extent to the restoration of union and harmony among themselves; much also appears to have been the result of various improvements in their armour and tactics which had been introduced by Camillus. They were further strengthened by a renewal of the alliance with Latium.

Rome was thus prepared for any emergency, and opportunities soon occurred in which it was decided whether Rome should become the mistress of Italy or not. The *Samnites*, the most powerful nation in Central Italy, came into conflict with Rome in B.C. 343. They had then been in alliance and on friendly terms with Rome for ten years. They had previously spread their influence over a great part of Southern Italy by colonising Capua, the plains of Campania, and Lucania, though in the course of time these colonies had become estranged from the mother country. The manner in which they became involved in war with Rome is related as follows. The Samnites were engaged in hostilities against the Sidicines, who, being too weak, applied to Capua for assistance. Capua willingly granted the request, but was defeated by the Samnites in two battles. In its distress Capua applied to Rome for help; but as the Romans hesitated to support strangers against the Samnites, their own allies, Capua offered to recognise the supremacy of Rome, if she would grant the request. Rome at once accepted the offer, and resolved to send succour to Capua. From this account we might expect hereafter to find Capua in the condition of a city subject to Rome; but such is not the case, and the truth is that the above story is a mere invention to disguise the fact that Rome had violated her treaty with Samnium. The war which thus broke out and lasted from B.C. 343 to B.C. 341, is only the first in a series of wars which were destined to decide which of the two nations was to have the supremacy in Italy. In the first campaign the Romans, led on by Valerius Corvus, gained an important victory on Mount Gaurus. A second army, destined to invade Samnium, allowed itself to be drawn into a position among the mountains, where it would have been utterly destroyed, had it not been saved by the boldness and skill of the plebeian military tribune *Decius Mus*, who contrived to gain possession of an eminence overhanging the enemy, and thus enabled the Roman army to pass safely through the defile. In the second year of the war, nothing of any importance was achieved, and as the Latins showed symptoms of dissatisfaction, and disturbances broke out in Rome itself in consequence of the severe law of debt, the Romans thought it prudent to stop the war and renew the old alliance with the Samnites.

The inhabitants of Capua, thus finding themselves forsaken by the Romans, now sought an alliance with the Latins. In order to meet this fresh danger, the Romans at once, in B.C. 340, commenced hostile operations against the Latins. The latter, unwilling to take up arms against Rome, with which they had been allied so long, now demanded that Rome and Latium should be really united into one state, for hitherto the Romans had always more or less domineered over the Latins, though they were allies on equal terms. The Latins further demanded that one of the consuls and one-half of the senators should always be taken from the Latins. These demands, though they were not unreasonable, created such exasperation at Rome that war was declared at once. The war was carried on in Campania, and a great battle was fought at the foot of Mount Vesuvius, in which *Publius Decius Mus*, one of the consuls, caused himself to be devoted to death by a priest, and then furiously rushed among the Latins until he himself was slain. He thus sacrificed himself in the hope of thereby securing the victory to his countrymen. During the same campaign *Manlius Torquatus* exhibited an example of severity which was revolting even to the Romans themselves. Orders had been given that no soldier should engage in fighting out of his own line; but Manlius, a son of Torquatus, being taunted and provoked by a haughty Latin, was unable to control his anger and slew him. Rejoiced at his victory, he carried the spoils of his enemy to his father, who, to punish his disobedience, ordered him to be put to death. The friends of young Manlius procured a splendid funeral for him, and the unnatural father was ever after shunned and detested for this excess of severity.

After the first defeat of the Latins, they were deserted by Capua, which made its peace with Rome on favourable terms. But the Latins continued the war with unabated vigour, until after another defeat in the second campaign the Latin confederacy broke up, in consequence of which most of the towns surrendered one after the other. Their example was followed by the Volscians, so that in B.C. 338 the subjugation of the Latins and Volscians was completed. Rome, however, treated the conquered people with moderation, for some of the towns received the full Roman franchise, while others obtained the franchise without the suffrage, or became Roman municipia—that is, towns whose internal administration was independent of Rome. Some important towns, however, whose resistance had been most formidable, were weakened by their best families being sent into exile, and by being deprived of a portion of their territory. Every Latin town, moreover, was isolated as much as possible from the others by a regulation that no person of one town was allowed to marry into another, or possess property in another. Rome thus secured for ever her power over the whole of Latium, and further strengthened her rule by the establishment of colonies in the conquered countries, which were in reality military garrisons, and generally received one-third of the landed property of the original inhabitants.

We have already mentioned that during the first Samnite war the internal peace of Rome had been disturbed by the severity of the law of debt. In the very year before the termination of the Latin war, B.C. 339, the dictator, *Publilius Philo*, carried three important laws, the first of which abolished the veto which the patrician comitia curiata had possessed on all legal enactments passed by the comitia centuriata; the second law gave to the decrees of the comitia tributa the full power of laws binding on the whole nation; and the third enacted that one of the censors should always be a plebeian. The last patrician privileges thus gradually disappeared one after another; and the Roman republic now consisted of citizens, all of whom possessed equal rights. The Latins and the allies, as they were termed, though in reality they were subjects of Rome, had to provide the greater part of the armies in the wars of the great city against her enemies.

THE CAPITOLINE TEMPLE.

CHAPTER IV.

FROM THE SUBJUGATION OF LATIUM TO THAT OF ALL ITALY.

B.C. 338 to B.C. 272.

THE great increase of power recently acquired by the Romans appears to have excited the jealousy of the Samnites; and the Romans becoming aware of this, endeavoured to strengthen themselves still more, partly by alliances with other Italian nations, and partly by the establishment of colonies on or near the frontiers of Samnium. One of these colonies, sent out in B.C. 328, was established on the site of Fregellæ, a Volscian town which had been taken and destroyed by the Samnites. As the territory thus belonged to the Samnites, they remonstrated with, and even threatened, Rome; and when, two years later, the Samnites supported Neapolis (Naples) in its war against Rome, the latter at once declared war. Neapolis soon after concluded peace with Rome, while Lucania, which had been allied with Rome, now joined the Samnites, who further received the support of Tarentum. Hostilities were commenced in Apulia, where the Romans conquered some towns which were in alliance with Samnium, and afterwards gained a decisive victory. The Samnites were thereby induced to ask for a truce of one year, which was granted; but at the end of it a body of Samnites invaded Latium while the Roman army was still engaged in Apulia. Rome was in imminent danger, but as most of the Latin towns remained faithful, the enemy was driven back; and in Apulia, too, the Roman arms were successful. The Samnites offered to treat for peace, but the demands of the Romans were so exorbitant that the Samnites were unable to comply with them, and they now made every effort to defend their independence. In B.C. 321, the Romans, by the careless management of their consuls, Veturius and Postumius, lost nearly all the advantages they had gained in their previous campaigns. Their army was surrounded on all sides in the mountain pass of *Caudium*, and being defeated in a terrible battle, was compelled to surrender. All those who escaped death on that day had to pass under the yoke, and the Samnite commander *Pontius* generously offered them fair terms of peace. The conditions were accepted by the Roman commanders, and the army was allowed to return home. But the Roman senate haughtily refused to ratify the peace, and sent back in chains those who had concluded it. Pontius declined to receive them, and the war was continued by the Romans with the greatest vigour, to wipe off the disgrace of Caudium; and henceforth the Roman annals are full of accounts of brilliant victories over the Samnites; but one of their commanders, *Fabius Maximus*, was defeated in a hotly contested battle at Lautulæ, in consequence of which Rome lost several of her allied towns. However, the sufferings of the Samnites were daily increasing, and their strength diminishing. They were defeated in several engagements, while Campania and Apulia were obliged to submit to Rome, which might now easily have crushed the Samnites, had not fresh dangers arisen in other quarters.

In B.C. 311, the Etruscans, who had long looked upon Rome's growing power with uneasiness, took up arms against her, and thus obliged her to divide her forces. In consequence of this, the Roman armies in the south suffered a great defeat near Allifæ, and in Samnium their legions found themselves in great distress. However, *Papirius Cursor*, who was appointed dictator in B.C. 309, so completely routed the Samnites, that they were compelled to take to flight, leaving their camp in the hands of the enemy. Meanwhile a great coalition of the Marsians, Pelignians, Umbrians, Hernicans, and Æquians, was formed against Rome. The Umbrians were soon reduced to submission by Fabius Maximus, the war against the Etruscans was near its end, and the Hernicans were easily overpowered, so that the Romans being enabled to direct all their forces against the Samnites, put them to flight in all directions, B.C. 306. The coalition on which the Samnites had relied being now broken up, and their own armies defeated, they concluded a truce, in the hope of obtaining peace on tolerable terms. But their hopes were disappointed, for after the expiration of the truce, the Romans laid waste Samnium in all directions; and when, in B.C. 305, they suffered a further defeat, their power was completely crushed. Samnium was now obliged to accept the terms dictated by Rome: it had to give up the supremacy over Lucania, to renounce its alliance with other Italian nations, and, in fact, to concede to the Romans to interfere in all their foreign relations. This humiliating peace concluded the second Samnite war, in B.C. 304, having lasted twenty-four years.

The Hernicans, who had been easily reduced to submission in B.C. 306, experienced on the whole the same fate as the Latins. The Æquians rashly rose against Rome at a time when she had already concluded peace with Samnium, and they had to pay the penalty of seeing their towns conquered or destroyed one after another. The Etruscans also had begun their war too late, and after it had lasted for some years, their cities, in B.C. 308, began to conclude peace with Rome each for itself for a fixed number of years. During these wars Rome had made a treaty with Tarentum, in which it was stipulated that no Roman ships should sail beyond Cape Lacinium.

The short period following the conclusion of the peace with the Samnites was employed by the Romans in consolidating their power in the newly conquered countries. The Samnites, on the other hand, were only waiting for a favourable opportunity to recommence hostilities. Such an opportunity presented itself in the disturbed state of Lucania, over which they hoped to recover their supremacy. The nobility of that country, being at war with the people, placed themselves under the protection of the Romans, who at once called upon the Samnites to withdraw from Lucania, and not to interfere in its affairs. This demand produced such exasperation among the Samnites, that war was forthwith declared in B.C. 298. At the same time, the Etruscans again rose in arms, allied themselves with the Umbrians, and even called in the aid of Gallic mercenaries. During the first two years, the Samnites were defeated in several great battles, and their country was fearfully ravaged; and in the third all Lucania was recovered by the Romans. The Etruscans received assistance from the Samnites; but all was of no avail, for the Roman arms were victorious everywhere. One thing only alarmed the Romans, viz., a report that large bodies of Gauls, supported by the Etruscans and Umbrians, were coming southward. Incredible efforts were made to meet the threatening danger. At first the Romans suffered several reverses in Etruria, but the arrival of the consuls changed the course of events. A great battle was fought near *Sentinum*, in Umbria, which would have been lost, had not *Decius*, one of the consuls, caused himself and the hostile army to be devoted to the infernal gods. This self-sacrifice gave fresh spirit to the Romans, and enabled them to gain a brilliant victory. The Samnite army which had been sent to support the Etruscans, was cut to pieces, and 25,000 Gauls and Samnites covered the field of battle, while 8000 were made prisoners. Fabius then proceeded from Umbria into Etruria, where he gained another victory over the Etruscans near Perusia.

While these things were going on in the north of Italy, a Samnite army, which was ravaging Campania, is said to have been defeated with great loss by the Romans returning from Sentinum. In the year B.C. 294, the Etruscan towns found it advisable to conclude peace with Rome. But the Samnites made most desperate efforts, and having called out all their men capable of bearing arms, invaded Campania. The Romans compelled them to return by attacking Samnium, from which they carried off a vast amount of booty. Upon this, the Samnites, under their brave and noble commander, *Pontius*, again invaded Campania. The Romans were at first unsuccessful; but in B.C. 292, the aged *Fabius Maximus* fought a fierce battle, which at once decided the contest between Rome and Samnium: 20,000 Samnites were killed, and 4000 made prisoners, one of whom was the brave Pontius. He was taken to Rome in triumph and beheaded—an act of base ingratitude towards a man who had saved the Roman army at Caudium. Hostilities, however, continued until B.C. 290, when the Samnites sued for peace, which was granted to them on condition of their acknowledging the supremacy of Rome. Soon afterwards, the Umbrians, Etruscans, and two Keltic tribes, the Senones and Boians, had to submit to the same terms. Rome had now acquired the dominion of the whole of Central Italy, the submission of which was secured as usual by the establishment of numerous colonies.

If we now turn our attention from these successful wars to the internal affairs of Rome, we find that during the same period she became internally more and more consolidated by the equalisation of the two orders, and that many useful works were executed in and about the city for the public convenience. In the year B.C. 312, the censor *Appius Claudius* made the famous Appian road, leading from Rome to Capua (it was afterwards continued to Brundisium), and the first aqueduct which supplied Rome with water. In the same year a kind of calendar was set up in public, informing the people on what days it was lawful to administer justice and to hold public meetings. A great constitutional change appears to have been made about the same time, by which the comitia centuriata were combined with the comitia tributa, although the latter still continued to be convened separately as before. In B.C. 300, the tribune *Ogulnius* proposed and carried a law by which the number of pontiffs and augurs was increased to eight and nine respectively, and by which it was enacted that one-half of these priestly colleges should be taken from the plebeians. Henceforth all the public offices possessing political power were equally divided between patricians and plebeians. The agrarian law of Licinius Stolo was never repealed, but appears to have been repeatedly violated with impunity, and the distribution of public land among the poorer citizens was rarely resorted to, though many must have suffered greatly in consequence of the protracted wars at a distance from Rome. But notwithstanding these drawbacks, Rome was now entering upon a period of her history which may be regarded as the beginning of her golden age.

The peace which Rome enjoyed after the termination of the Samnite wars was interrupted by renewed attacks of the Gauls and Etruscans. The war against the former, beginning in B.C. 285, was brought to a close in B.C. 282 by the total subjugation of the Senones and Boii. The Etruscans continued in arms for a few years longer, but ultimately obtained a peace on very favourable terms, in consequence of which they made no further attempts to recover their independence, and seem to have enjoyed a considerable degree of prosperity under the dominion of Rome.

Tarentum, a powerful commercial and manufacturing Greek city in the south of Italy, was looking with uneasiness upon the growing power of the Romans in the south. Like all commercial states, it chiefly relied upon mercenaries, and endeavoured to keep Rome engaged by inducing other nations to take up arms against her. Thus they are said to have instigated the Etruscans in their last contest. They even induced the Samnites to join in a coalition against the common enemy. The first act of hostility consisted in the Lucanians attacking Thurii, a

Greek city allied with Rome; but the town was relieved by Caius Fabricius, in B.C. 282, who also gained other advantages over the southern confederates. As the Romans were obliged to keep up communication with Thurii by sea, they could not help violating the treaty with Tarentum, which forbade them to sail beyond Cape Lacinium. When, therefore, ten Roman ships were seen sailing towards the harbour of Tarentum, a Tarentine fleet immediately sailed out to attack them, and captured five of the Roman ships. The Tarentines even went so far as to compel Thurii to open its gates to them. The Roman senate, indignant at such proceedings, sent an embassy to remonstrate and demand reparation; but the Tarentines treated the ambassadors with contempt and insult, so that war became unavoidable. The Tarentines had hoped to bring about a general coalition among the southern Italians; but failing in this, they invited Pyrrhus, king of Epirus, to come to their assistance.

Pyrrhus, whose mind was full of an adventurous and chivalrous spirit, gladly accepted the invitation in the hope of acquiring a great empire by adding Italy and Sicily to his dominions. When, in B.C. 281, he arrived with his forces at Tarentum, he at once set about drilling its citizens, and compelling them to submit to severe military discipline. It was this new danger which induced the Romans to conclude the final peace with the Etruscans on favourable terms, and they now sent out armies both against the Samnites and the Tarentines. The hostile forces met on the banks of the little river *Siris;* and Pyrrhus, partly by means of his well-trained Macedonian soldiers, and partly by the terror inspired by his elephants, which the Romans had never seen employed in war, gained a decisive victory over his enemies. This first success induced many of the southern Italians openly to join Pyrrhus. But as he himself had sustained very severe losses in the battle, he sent his friend Cineas to Rome to offer peace. The Roman senate refused to listen to any proposals so long as Pyrrhus and his army remained in Italy. Upon this the king advanced northward to the very neighbourhood of Rome, but finding that the Etruscans could no longer be calculated upon, he returned to Tarentum. In B.C. 279, the Roman consuls again met their enemy near *Asculum*, where Pyrrhus again won a great victory. But his losses were so great that he is reported to have said, "One more such victory, and I shall be undone." He expressed his admiration of the valour of the Romans by saying, "If I had such soldiers, the world would be mine."

The Romans after these two defeats felt inclined to come to terms with Pyrrhus, but Appius Claudius most strenuously opposed such policy, so long as Pyrrhus refused to quit Italy. The king himself despaired of the Greeks of Southern Italy, while the Romans had filled him with admiration. In these circumstances he readily accepted an invitation of the Sicilian Greeks, who hoped with his assistance to drive the Carthaginians out of the island. A truce was accordingly concluded with Rome, and in B.C. 278 he proceeded to Sicily. The friends and allies he found there he soon discovered to be even less trustworthy than those of Italy, for nearly all his undertakings were thwarted by their faithless and treacherous disposition, in consequence of which he was led into several acts of cruelty. Finding at last that nothing great could be effected in the island, and that his Italian allies were hard pressed by the Romans during his absence, he returned to Italy after an absence of three years. Meanwhile the Romans had punished their revolted allies and subjects, and many a victory had been gained by them. On his arrival he recovered indeed several towns which had been lost, and then proceeded towards Beneventum, where the consul *Curius Dentatus* was encamped; but his army being no longer what it had been, was there so completely defeated, in B.C. 275, that he escaped to Tarentum with only a few horsemen. He had applied to some of the eastern powers for assistance, but as his request was not complied with, he at once resolved to quit Italy, leaving only a small garrison at Tarentum.

After his departure, the Tarentines concluded peace with the Romans, who, within the next few years, compelled the Samnites, Lucanians, and Bruttians, to do homage to the republic of Rome, which was now the virtual mistress of all Italy from the northern frontier of Etruria to the Straits of Sicily. The only nation which could not meekly submit to Rome were the Samnites, who, in B.C. 268, once more took up arms to defend their independence; but their fate was finally decided in the very first campaign.

The conquered nations were treated differently according as they had shown more or less hostility during the wars; but all had to recognise the supremacy of Rome, which, as usual, secured its conquests by the establishment of numerous colonies. As many of the southern Italians were good sailors and possessed fleets, Rome now was in a position to carry on wars with any nation beyond the sea, with which she might come in contact. She had now become one of the great states of the time, and might have limited herself to the dominion of Italy and united the whole of it into one compact state with free institutions. But circumstances soon occurred which rendered such a scheme, if it ever existed, a matter of impossibility.

A YOUNG ROMAN IN THE TOGA.

ARIES, OR BATTERING-RAM.

CHAPTER V.

FROM THE CONQUEST OF ALL ITALY DOWN TO THE OUTBREAK OF THE SECOND PUNIC WAR.

B.C. 272 TO B.C. 218.

IN the very first year of the republic, B.C. 509, Rome had concluded a commercial treaty with the wealthy city of *Carthage*, a Phœnician colony on the north coast of Africa. The same treaty had been twice renewed, and the relation between the two republics had always been of an amicable kind, but during the conquests of the Romans in Southern Italy the Carthaginians seem to have become apprehensive of the growing power of Rome. When Pyrrhus was in Sicily with the avowed object of driving the Carthaginians from the island, they concluded a defensive alliance with Rome which was directed against their common enemy, although in the war against him they never united their forces. When Pyrrhus withdrew from Sicily, the island fell into a complete state of anarchy; and a body of Campanian mercenaries, called *Mamertines*, ravaged the country and took forcible possession of Messana, where they murdered or expelled the male population, and distributed their property as well as their wives and children among themselves. The Syracusans, under the command of their King Hiero, attacked these lawless marauders, and reduced them to such straits as to oblige them to look about for foreign assistance. One party thought of calling in the aid of the Carthaginians, who had already offered their assistance, and took possession of the citadel of Messana; but the majority solicited the assistance of Rome. Six years before this, the Romans had most severely punished a body of Campanian mercenaries, who had acted at Rhegium in the same manner as the Mamertines had done at Messana. The better part of the Roman senate therefore seem to have felt that it would be scarcely decent to support such a band of robbers as the Mamertines. The matter was, however, referred to the popular assembly, with whom the love of war and conquest stifled every other feeling. An alliance was accordingly concluded with the Mamertines; and Hiero, finding himself powerless against them, made his peace with them. Every pretext for Roman interference was thus removed, but the opportunity of making war against Carthage was too tempting, and a message was sent to Messana to inform the Mamertines that Rome was ready to deliver them from the Carthaginians. A fleet furnished by the Greek maritime towns of Southern Italy sailed across from Rhegium, and on its arrival the Carthaginian commander of Messana treacherously surrendered the citadel to the Romans. The Carthaginians, however, demanded that the Romans should quit Sicily, and as this was refused, they, supported by King Hiero, laid siege to Messana. Meanwhile fresh legions arrived in Sicily, and defeated Hiero before he could obtain assistance from his allies. Hereupon Hiero withdrew to Syracuse, and in B.C. 263 concluded a peace with the Romans, to whom ever after he remained a most faithful friend. The Carthaginians being likewise beaten, dispersed among their subject towns in the western parts of the island.

The Romans are said to have been enormously successful in Sicily, and sixty-seven towns are reported to have surrendered to them. As the Carthaginians did not make any stand against the invaders, the conquest of the whole island seemed to be a matter of no great difficulty. But in B.C. 262, the Romans found that Agrigentum, which they were besieging, was not so easily conquered, for it took them seven months to compel the city to surrender. Its numerous Carthaginian garrison escaped, but the city had to endure all the horrors of a place taken by the sword. As Carthage with its powerful fleet was the undisputed mistress of the sea, the Roman senate ordered a fleet to be built in all haste after the model of a Carthaginian ship, which had been wrecked on the coast of Bruttium. The command of this fleet was entrusted, in B.C. 260, to *Caius Duilius*, and in the ensuing engagement off Mylæ, he changed the naval battle into a sort of land fight by means of boarding bridges thrown upon the enemy's ships. Although the Romans had hitherto had no experience in maritime warfare, their victory, partly owing to their extraordinary contrivance, was so complete, that the Carthaginians were obliged to take to flight, having lost about 10,000 men in killed and wounded. The Romans afterwards honoured Duilius, by erecting to him a column adorned with the beaks of captured ships, and with an inscription recording the details of his victory. Elated by their first success at sea, they determined to drive the Carthaginians from all their insular possessions in the west of the Mediterranean, and expeditions were at once undertaken against Sardinia and Corsica. The operations in Sicily were in the meantime carried on with less vigour, whereby the Carthaginians were enabled to gain some advantages; but in B.C. 258 the consul *Atilius Calatinus* restored the honour of the Roman arms; and the town of Myttistratum, which had been besieged by the Romans for some time, was now abandoned by its garrison, and fell into their hands. The same was the case with several other towns.

But although the Romans were thus far successful, one-half of Sicily was still occupied by the Carthaginians. In B.C. 256, the Romans resolved to carry the war into **Africa**; with immense exertions they prepared a fleet of

330 ships, which, under the command of *Manlius* and *Atilius Regulus*, were to steer towards the African coast. Near Ecnomus, the Romans were met by a still larger fleet of the Carthaginians, and a fearful battle ensued, in which the Carthaginians were so completely defeated, that they felt induced to make offers of peace. These offers, however, were rejected, and the Roman fleet, proceeding to Africa, landed near Clupea, which, being deserted by its inhabitants, was occupied by the Romans as their headquarters. The country was ravaged by the invaders in all directions, and when at the close of the year Manlius returned to Italy with a portion of the army, and a large number of prisoners, Regulus with his diminished forces began the campaign of B.C. 255, by besieging the town of Adis, and it is said that both this and many other towns submitted to him. The Carthaginians were so much reduced as to be obliged to retreat within the walls of their own city. In this distress, they sent to Regulus to sue for peace, but, though he might now have concluded the war in an honourable manner, he proposed such humiliating terms, that the Carthaginians resolved to die sword in hand rather than submit to the insolence of their enemy.

In these circumstances, Carthage was fortunate in securing the services of one of those Greek soldiers, who at that time offered their services to any one who chose to employ them. This was the Spartan *Xanthippus*, to whom they at once entrusted the command of their forces. He set about increasing and reorganising the army, and by improving their discipline, inspired the men with fresh confidence. In his first encounter with the Romans, he routed and dispersed the whole Roman army, and Regulus himself with 500 men was taken prisoner. About 2000 escaped to Clupea, where they defended themselves bravely. The Roman fleet which came to their rescue gained a brilliant victory over the Carthaginians and rescued them. But the same fleet, on its return to Sicily, was overtaken by a storm in which most of the ships were wrecked, and the south coast of

Sicily was covered with corpses and the fragments of the ships. This inspired the Carthaginians with fresh courage; but the Romans also, far from being disheartened, in B.C. 254, prepared a new fleet of 220 ships, with which they sailed to Sicily, and took several towns, while others surrendered of their own accord. But still as their progress was slow, they again sailed to Africa and laid waste its coast districts. On its return to Sicily, when they had just come in sight of Cape Palinurus, a violent storm overtook the fleet, and no less than 150 ships were wrecked. This second disaster at sea discouraged the Romans to such a degree, that they resolved henceforth to keep no more ships than were necessary to protect Italy and convey troops to Sicily.

The Romans, notwithstanding, continued to make progress during the following years, and succeeded in confining the Carthaginians to the western corner of Sicily. In B.C. 250 the Roman consul *Cæcilius* defeated the Carthaginians in a great battle near Panormus, which was the last great battle that was fought in this war. Having lost all their possessions in Sicily with the exception of the two fortresses of Lilybæum and Drepana, the Carthaginians were desirous of peace and to obtain an exchange of prisoners. They accordingly sent Regulus, who was still in captivity among them, to Rome for the purpose of proposing terms of peace, or at least to effect an exchange of prisoners. But Regulus, instead of fulfilling the duties of his mission, persuaded the senate to enter into no negotiations, and to continue the war. The Romans, notwithstanding their previous resolution, again built a fleet of 200 ships and began the siege of Lilybæum, which lasted for a long time. In B.C. 249, the Romans, under their haughty and presumptuous commander *Appius Claudius*, were defeated both by land and by sea, in the neighbourhood of Drepana, and the Carthaginians followed up their victory with great vigour. About the same time a vast number of Roman transports were destroyed in a storm, and those which escaped fell into the hands of the enemy. After this disaster, the Romans again renounced the sea, of which the Carthaginians were now again the undisputed masters. Carthage, moreover, had now the good fortune of having for its military chief the great *Hamilcar*, the father of Hannibal, who, in B.C. 247, undertook the command of the Carthaginian forces in Sicily. After some ravaging descents on the coast of Italy, he took up a strong position on Mount Hercte, whence he did incalculable damage to his enemies by frequent sallies. Afterwards he took up a similar position on Mount Eryx, whence he continued to harass the Romans, although he himself was surrounded by all manner of difficulties.

In this way the war was carried on without any decisive advantage being gained by either party. The Romans, having come to the conviction that the war could not be brought to a close without some extraordinary exertion, once more resolved, in B.C. 242, to build a new fleet. But as the treasury lacked the funds necessary for such an undertaking, the money was furnished by wealthy and patriotic citizens. An armada of 200 ships, commanded by *Lutatius Catulus*, having first made an unsuccessful attack upon Drepana, resolved to offer battle to the Carthaginian fleet. The latter, containing a large number of transports, was unable to cope with that of the Romans, and was easily and completely defeated; sixty-three of the enemy's ships were taken, one hundred and twenty were sunk, and the number of killed and prisoners was immense. This decisive victory was gained in B.C. 241, off the Ægatian islands. The Carthaginians were now compelled to sue for peace, which they obtained on the following conditions: that they should evacuate Sicily and the islands between it and Carthage, that they should abstain from war against Hiero and his allies, that they should restore all Roman prisoners without ransom, and pay 2300 talents in ten yearly instalments.

Thus terminated the First Punic War, which had been carried on by both parties with incredible efforts and losses, and Sicily was the first country out of Italy conquered by the Romans. The island was treated differently from the conquests hitherto made in Italy—it became a *Roman province*, that is, a country governed by a Roman prætor or pro-consul, who was sent out every year with supreme civil and military powers, and was assisted in the administration by a quæstor or treasurer. The revenues derived from a province were not levied by government officials, but were farmed by wealthy capitalists (*publicani*) or companies of them. The Sicilian towns and cities were not all treated in the same way, and a difference was made according to the degree of hostility they had shown in the war preceding the conquest. Thus in Sicily the kingdom of Hiero and several other towns remained perfectly free and independent. It is very remarkable that during the long period of the war with Carthage the Italian nations remained tranquil, and no attempt was made to shake off the yoke of Rome.

After the termination of the war, Carthage found herself in the greatest distress, and not being able to pay her mercenaries, they rose in open rebellion against her. This led to a war between Carthage and the rebellious soldiery which lasted upwards of three years, and was carried on by both parties with unexampled cruelty. The great Hamilcar at last succeeded in defeating the rebels. During this conflict the Romans behaved honourably towards their vanquished enemy, for they not only refused to countenance the rebels, but protected the transports of provisions destined for Carthage. But they changed their policy when the mercenaries in Sardinia likewise revolted; for when they applied to Rome for assistance, they eagerly seized the opportunity of taking possession of the island, B.C. 238. When Carthage remonstrated with them for this arbitrary proceeding, the Romans, with flagrant injustice, not only refused to listen to their demands, but took possession of the islands of Corsica and Sardinia, and demanded of Carthage the additional sum of 1200 talents. Carthage was too much exhausted to offer any resistance, but treasured up her indignation for a more convenient time, and Hamilcar at once began to make preparations to indemnify his country and to gain the means of avenging the wrong done to it.

The Romans, after taking possession of Corsica and Sardinia, found the natives less inclined to bear their yoke, than they had borne that of the Carthaginians, and accordingly became involved in long and tedious wars with them. About the same time they had to contend against the Ligurians and Boians, in the north of Italy; and while they were still engaged in these troublesome wars, another struggle was commenced, in B.C. 229, against the pirates of Illyricum, who were then governed by Queen Teuta, and were a scourge to the maritime towns of Greece. The Romans had no difficulty in conquering the semi-barbarous pirates, and several of the Greek places, such as Corcyra, Epidamnus, and Apollonia placed themselves under the protection of Rome, which thus, for the first time, gained a footing on the continent of Greece. Even Athens and Corinth showed their gratitude to the Romans by conferring certain distinctions upon them.

But such wars as these against the Ligurians and Boians were trifling compared with that which burst upon the Romans about the same time from the north. The Boians, wincing under their subjection to Rome, and vexed that a portion of their territory which had become Roman domain land, had been given to Roman citizens by an agrarian law, invited other Gauls to join them in a fresh war against Rome. Even Gauls from beyond the Alps were induced to assist the Boians. In B.C. 226, formidable hosts of Gauls came across the Alps, and as they moved southward, the Romans were panic-stricken, for the barbarians devastated everything by fire and sword; but when they had advanced as far as Clusium they met the Romans, whom they nearly surrounded and annihilated. However, the Romans gained a decisive victory over the invaders near Telamon on the coast of Etruria, in which 40,000 Gauls are said to have been killed and 10,000 taken prisoners. This was the most memorable success the Romans had ever met with against the Gauls, and in consequence of it the Boians, in the year after the battle, B.C. 224, were forced to submit;

and the Romans for the first time crossed over to the northern banks of the Po, where, in the year B.C. 223, the consul Caius Flaminius fought a successful battle against the Insubrians. This war against the Gauls was brought to a close in B.C. 222 by *Claudius Marcellus* in the battle of Clastidium, where he slew the Gallic chief Viridomarus with his own hand. A peace was then concluded, in which the Gauls had to recognise the supremacy of Rome, and by which Rome acquired the extensive and fertile plains of Lombardy, which they endeavoured to secure by the establishment of the colonies of Placentia and Cremona.

While the Roman arms were thus engaged in the north of Italy, the Illyrians, instigated by Demetrius of Pharos, had renewed their piratical practices. But the consul Æmilius Paulus, in B.C. 219, finally stopped their proceedings by subduing the whole of Illyricum. Demetrius, however, escaped to the court of Philip, king of Macedonia, who had already been jealously watching the influence which the Romans had gained in the affairs of Greece.

After the loss of the islands in the Mediterranean, the Carthaginians, guided by the wise counsels of their great general *Hamilcar*, endeavoured to indemnify themselves by making conquests and forming a new empire in Spain, and by a wise moderation and kind treatment Hamilcar succeeded in winning the affection of many of the natives. After some years of successful operations, he was killed in a battle, B.C. 229, leaving the command of his army to *Hasdrubal*, his son-in-law, who continued the policy of his predecessor, and founded the town of New Carthage. The progress made by the Carthaginians in Spain somewhat alarmed the Romans, and in a treaty which they concluded with Hasdrubal, but which was never sanctioned by the government at Carthage, it was stipulated that the Carthaginians should not carry their conquests beyond the river Iberus. Hasdrubal was murdered in B.C. 221, and was succeeded in the command of the army by the great *Hannibal*, the son of Hamilcar, who, when only nine years old, had accompanied his father into

Spain and was trained under his immediate guidance. He is said even at that early age to have sworn eternal enmity to the Romans.

Immediately after undertaking the command of the army he continued the conquest begun by his predecessors, and subdued Spain as far as the river Iberus with the exception of the town of Saguntum, which is said to have been allied with Rome. Some disputes between that town and its neighbours afforded him an opportunity of commencing hostilities against it, and in B.C. 219 he proceeded to besiege the place. When Roman ambassadors called upon him to abstain from hostilities against the town, he referred them to the senate at Carthage. But there the ambassadors were equally unsuccessful, for although the aristocratic party wished to maintain peace with Rome under all circumstances, the popular party and the friends of Hannibal refused to take their great general to account or to recall him. Fabius, the spokesman of the embassy, then making a fold of his toga, said, "Here I bring you peace and war: take whichever you please." When the Carthaginians replied, "Give us whichever you please," he replied, "Well, then, I offer you war." This settled the question, and war was declared at once. In the meantime the Saguntines defended themselves most bravely against the besiegers, but after eight months of a most heroic resistance, the town was taken and destroyed. The inhabitants were partly buried under the ruins of their own houses, and partly killed themselves by leaping into the fire which they had kindled in the market place to destroy their remaining property. All the survivors were put to the sword. This war against Saguntum was only a prelude to the Second Punic War, which was carried on in Italy and brought to a close in Africa.

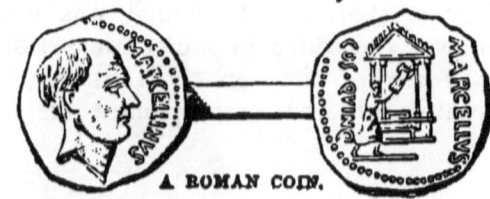

A ROMAN COIN.

HANNIBAL.

CHAPTER VI.

FROM THE SECOND PUNIC WAR DOWN TO THE END OF THE WAR AGAINST ANTIOCHUS.

B.C. 218 TO B.C. 188.

WHEN the Romans declared war against Carthage, they had only just brought to a close that against the Gauls, and were still engaged in Illyricum, whence they were unable to act with that decision and quickness which they usually displayed. Hannibal assembled his troops at New Carthage, and leaving the command in Spain to his brother Hasdrubal, proceeded in the spring of B.C. 218 to the river Iberus, which he crossed with an army of 90,000 foot, 12,000 horse, and 37 elephants. When he reached the Pyrenees, he gave leave to all those who felt disinclined to accompany him on his great expedition to return home. Large numbers availed themselves of this permission, and his forces were reduced to 50,000 foot and 9000 horse, but all were men determined to follow their great chief. On his march through Gaul he met with little or no opposition until he reached the river Rhone, the passage of which he had to force against hosts of Gauls drawn up on the opposite bank. When this was effected, he began his memorable march up the Alps, which he crossed by the Little St Bernard amid indescribable and overwhelming difficulties. When he descended on the south side of the Alps, his forces were reduced to 20,000 foot and 6000 horse. The passage of the Alps had been effected in fifteen days, and his arrival in Italy was hailed by the Gauls who hoped that he would deliver them from the detested yoke of Rome.

Meanwhile the Romans, on hearing of Hannibal's design to march across the Alps, had sent the consul *Publius Cornelius Scipio* with an army and fleet into Gaul, while his colleague, Sempronius Longus, proceeded with another army to Sicily. When Scipio arrived in Gaul, Hannibal had already crossed the Rhone, and, after a trifling engagement with a detachment of Hannibal's cavalry, he returned to Italy, where he arrived on the banks of the Po, when Hannibal had already descended from the Alps. The hostile armies first met on the river *Ticinus*, where Scipio was severely wounded, and afterwards on the river *Trebia*. In both of these places the Romans were defeated, and as the approach of winter put an end to further military operations, Hannibal remained in Lombardy. In the beginning of spring B.C. 217 he crossed the Appenines, and on the banks of Lake *Trasimenus* he was met by the consul Caius Flaminius, who intended to defend the road to Rome. A terrible battle was fought there on a foggy morning in which 15,000 Romans perished. The consul himself was among the slain, and a detachment which had been sent to his assistance was likewise cut to pieces. Hannibal had hoped by treating the Italians kindly to win them over to his side, but the Italian allies, and especially the Roman colonies, remained faithful; and when immediately after the battle of Lake Trasimenus he attacked Spoletium, he met with a determined resistance, and thus finding that he had miscalculated, he abandoned the place and marched along the eastern coast of Italy towards Apulia in the hope of stirring up the southern Italians against their Roman rulers.

The disaster of Lake Trasimenus had thrown Rome into a state of the greatest consternation. *Quintus Fabius Maximus,* surnamed Cunctator (the Slack), was at once appointed dictator, it being feared that the enemy would march straightway to Rome. Fabius finding that Hannibal had taken a different road, followed him as closely as he could with safety, and avoiding any decisive engagement, contrived to gain several smaller advantages. In the neighbourhood of Casilinum, Hannibal, through some mistake of his guide, was placed in so difficult a position that he extricated himself only by a stratagem: he ordered bundles of brushwood to be fastened to the horns of 2000 oxen, which were then driven in the night with the faggots in a blaze towards the Romans, who, terrified by the sight, abandoned their favourable position, and thereby enabled the enemy to escape. Hannibal spent the following winter in Apulia, greatly disappointed that none of the subjects of Rome had yet joined him. The Romans, dissatisfied with what they believed to be cowardice or unnecessary caution of Fabius, gave the consulship of the year B.C. 216 to *Terentius Varro* and *Æmilius Paulus.* The character of the former was the very opposite of that of Fabius, and the Romans expected that the consuls would put an end to the war at one blow. They proceeded to Apulia with a large army of 80,000 foot, and 6000 horse, and pitched their camp near the little town of *Cannæ.* The terrible defeat they suffered there showed, though too late, how wisely Fabius had acted, for no less than 47,000 Romans covered the field of battle, and the consul Æmilius Paulus and eighty senators were among the slain. Varro escaped with a few horsemen to Venusia.

Four battles had now been lost, but Rome, though humbled, did not despond, and proposals for peace or ransoming the prisoners were indignantly rejected. Hannibal, proceeding to Capua, was now joined by a number of Italians, who despaired of the fate of Rome; and Capua, one of the wealthiest cities of Italy, which had been treated by the Romans with great favour, openly declared for Hannibal. In that city he took up his winter quarters, and it is very remarkable that, although he had now gained numerous Italian allies and had received reinforcements from Africa, he gained no more great victories. The Romans made every effort to raise fresh troops, and even enlisted a body of 8000 slaves. In B.C. 215, commanded by Claudius Marcellus, they inflicted a severe blow upon Hannibal at Nola, and Tib. Sempronius Gracchus gained other advantages near Beneventum. Encouraged by these successes, they now laid siege to Capua, which Hannibal had abandoned. When, however, he found that the city was in danger, he advanced to its relief; but as the Romans declined a battle, he marched towards Rome and pitched his camp near its very gates. A portion of the army besieging Capua was despatched against him and offered battle; but Hannibal, for reasons not mentioned, contented himself with ravaging the country, and returned to the south of Italy.

Meanwhile King Hiero, the faithful ally of Rome, had died, and his successors entered into an alliance with Hannibal. In consequence of this, the Romans, in B.C. 214, sent *Claudius Marcellus* into Sicily, who at once laid siege to Syracuse. This siege lasted for two years, at the end of which the city was delivered up to the Romans by treachery. The Syracusans, assisted by the mechanical skill of the great mathematician *Archimedes*, defended themselves most gallantly, but were punished most severely by their conquerors. The splendour of Syracuse was destroyed for ever, and Archimedes was murdered while engaged in his scientific pursuits. All Sicily again fell into the hands of the Romans, and Hannibal endeavoured to indemnify himself by the conquest of Tarentum and some other places in Southern Italy. In the year 211, Capua was also retaken by the Romans, and its inhabitants were treated with wanton cruelty; twenty-seven senators committed suicide, and others killed their wives and children to save them from the insolence of the conquerors. Two years later Tarentum was recovered by Fabius Maximus. The treatment inflicted on Syracuse and Capua so much frightened the Italian Greeks that they thought it prudent to abandon their connection with Hannibal, whose only hope now rested on the succours which he expected from his brother Hasdrubal.

At the very commencement of the war in B.C. 218, the two brothers *Cneius* and *Publius Cornelius Scipio* had proceeded to Spain to operate against Hasdrubal, and for several years they harassed and checked his progress. At the same time they entered into negotiations with the African chief *Syphax* to attack Carthage itself. But in B.C. 212 both brothers fell in battle within thirty days of each other, and their armies were completely routed. Hasdrubal now formed the plan of joining his brother in Italy with fresh forces. The disasters suffered in Spain were so discouraging to the Romans that no one was willing to undertake the command of a new army there, until young *Publius Cornelius Scipio*, the son of one of the two Scipios who had fallen in Spain, though only twenty-four years old, offered to undertake the perilous task. On his arrival in Spain, in B.C. 211, affairs at once took a different turn, and in his second campaign he took New Carthage, the most important town of the Carthaginians. By his kindness and gentleness he attached the Spaniards to himself, and his popularity soon eclipsed that of Hasdrubal, who was defeated in B.C. 209 in a great battle near Bæcula. But Hasdrubal, notwithstanding this discomfiture, at length resolved to join his brother in Italy. In B.C. 207 he crossed the Alps and marched through the eastern part of Italy to meet his brother in Apulia. But on reaching the river Metaurus he met the consul Claudius Nero, who attacked him by night, while attempting to cross the river. Hasdrubal himself was killed, and his army entirely cut to pieces. A Roman soldier cut off his head, and when the army returned to Apulia, flung it into the camp of Hannibal. This was the first and only intelligence that Hannibal received of his brother's arrival and defeat.

After this, Hannibal confined himself to a defensive attitude in Bruttium, which still remained faithful to him.

He there maintained himself with the greatest boldness and heroism for several years, and whoever attacked him had to pay dearly for it. After Hasdrubal's departure from Spain, the Carthaginians, no longer able to cope with Scipio, were gradually driven out of the country, and the whole of the southern part of the peninsula was conquered by the Romans. Scipio remained in Spain for several years, and having concluded a treaty with Syphax, he returned to Rome, where, notwithstanding his youth, he was elected consul for the year B.C. 205. He at once proposed to attack Carthage in Africa; but the cautious senate, considering this somewhat presumptuous, assigned to him Sicily as his province, with permission to proceed to Africa, if he thought it advantageous to his country. The means placed at his disposal were very insufficient, but the enthusiasm all over Italy was so great, that he was plentifully provided with all he needed by voluntary contributions.

When everything was prepared, Scipio, in B.C. 204, crossed over into Africa. Syphax treacherously joined the Carthaginians, but the Romans were amply compensated by being joined by the Numidian king, Masinissa. With his assistance Scipio burned the camp of Syphax and his allies, among whom great havoc was made. The last hope of Carthage now rested on Hannibal, who was forthwith summoned to return home. He arrived there in B.C. 202, and soon after had an interview with Scipio, at which both were inclined to come to terms. But the people of Carthage, elated by the presence of their great general, resolved once more to try the fortune of war. The battle of *Zama*, in B.C. 202, at last decided the contest between the two nations. The Carthaginians, though fighting most bravely, lost the day, and the greater part of their army was destroyed. Hannibal himself escaped to Carthage with only a few followers, and advised the people to submit to necessity and accept the terms offered by Scipio. The advice was followed, and Carthage had to surrender all Roman deserters and prisoners without ransom, to give up its whole fleet with the exception of ten ships, to promise to abstain from war with any foreign state without the sanction of Rome, to pay the sum of 10,000 talents by fifty yearly instalments, and to indemnify Masinissa for the losses he had sustained. The peace was ratified at Rome the year after, and Scipio, who celebrated a splendid triumph, was honoured with the surname of Africanus.

After the conclusion of this peace, Hannibal remained at Carthage doing all he could to repair the losses which his country had sustained, by wise reforms. But the Romans, ever afraid of his influence, contrived to undermine his authority, so that at last even his own countrymen began to lose confidence in him, and the greatest general and statesman that Carthage ever had, was obliged, in B.C. 196, to quit his country as an exile. He proceeded to the court of *Antiochus*, king of Syria, whom he endeavoured to inspire with his unquenchable hatred of the Romans. The gains which Rome had made during the Second Punic War were very great, notwithstanding the battles they had lost and the devastations to which Italy had been exposed, for the southern part of Spain was conquered, and Carthage and Numidia were virtually in a state of dependence on Rome.

We have seen that *Philip*, king of Macedonia, had become uneasy at the influence which Rome after the Illyrian wars had acquired in the affairs of Greece. Demetrius of Pharos did his best to increase this feeling; and after the battle of Cannæ, when Rome seemed to be finally crushed, Philip concluded a treaty with Hannibal, in which the countries on the east of the Adriatic were promised to Philip, while Carthage was to rule over the countries west of the Adriatic. But the document containing the treaty fell into the hands of the Romans, who at once adopted measures to prevent the Macedonian from sending assistance to Hannibal. A petty war was thus carried on from B.C. 215 to 205, during which neither the Romans nor the Macedonians gained any great advantages. A peace was then concluded, though neither party intended to keep it; and Rome especially, being unable to carry on another war so long as Hannibal was in Italy, only wanted to gain time.

A second war against Macedonia broke out in B.C. 200, because Philip had ravaged the territory of Athens, which was in alliance with Rome. This war was at first carried on by the Romans with little energy, and Philip, supported by many of the Greeks, was favoured by fortune; but in B.C. 198, when *Quinctius Flamininus* undertook the command and boldly entered the enemy's country, things assumed a different aspect. Philip was completely beaten in the battle of *Cynoscephalæ*, and obliged to sue for peace, in which he had to recognise the independence of Greece, to give up a great part of his fleet, to pay a large sum of money, and to give hostages as a security for his future conduct. This peace was ratified in B.C. 197, and in the year following, Flamininus, to the intense delight of the Greeks assembled at the Isthmian games, proclaimed the freedom and independence of their country.

The enthusiasm of the Greeks for their liberators, however, soon subsided, for they made the discovery that what was called their freedom, was in reality only a change of masters. The Ætolians, who had fought on the side of the Romans against Macedonia, not considering themselves sufficiently rewarded for their services, invited *Antiochus* of Syria to wage war against the Romans. Their endeavours were seconded by Hannibal. Antiochus, who also felt himself personally aggrieved by the demand of the Romans to restore to independence the Greek states of Asia Minor, readily accepted the proposal, and in B.C. 192 crossed over with an army into Europe. But instead of following the advice of Hannibal, to ally himself with Philip and attack the Romans in Italy, he offended Philip and wasted his time in frivolous amusements in Eubœa, while the Romans rapidly advanced into Thessaly. Commanded by Acilius Glabrio, in B.C. 191 they met Antiochus and the Ætolians at *Thermopylæ*, where they put their enemies to flight without any great effort, and Antiochus himself hastily fled back into Asia.

The Ætolians asked and obtained peace, as the Romans were anxious to leave no enemy in their rear, while continuing the war against Antiochus.

The year after the battle of Thermopylæ, a Roman army of 20,000 men, under the command of Caius Lælius and Lucius Cornelius Scipio (who was accompanied by his brother Africanus), proceeded to Asia. As Antiochus refused to accept the terms offered by the Romans, a great battle was fought near Magnesia, in which the hosts of Asiatics were easily overpowered by the Roman legions. Antiochus then fled to Syria and sued for peace, which was granted to him on condition that he should give up all his possessions in Asia west of Mount Taurus, and all his ships of war, and pay a large sum of money as a war indemnity. He was further requested to deliver up Hannibal. The peace was not ratified at Rome until B C. 188. The countries thus ceded by Antiochus were distributed among the allies at Rome, for the time had not yet come when it was thought desirable to constitute them as Roman provinces. Hannibal, finding that his life was not safe in Syria, sought the protection of Prusias, king of Bithynia; but here too the Romans pursued him, and as Prusias was unable to protect him any longer, Hannibal put an end to his life by poison, B.C. 183. His conqueror, Scipio Africanus, died about the same time; he too had spent the last years of his life in a kind of exile, into which he had been driven partly by the jealousy of his enemies and partly by his own insolent and overbearing conduct.

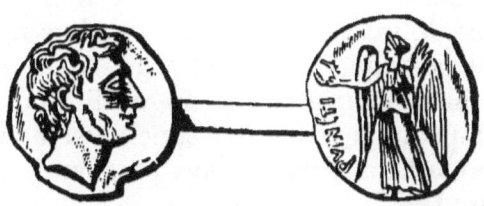

FLAMININUS.

SCIPIO AFRICANUS.

CHAPTER VII.

FROM THE PEACE WITH ANTIOCHUS DOWN TO THE TIME OF THE GRACCHI.

B.C. 188 TO B.C. 133.

WHILE these things were going on in the East, the peace of Italy had been disturbed by the insurrection of some of the Keltic tribes in the north, which continued their hostilities from B.C. 200 until B.C. 181, when the Kelts were finally compelled to submit to Rome. During this war the Boians seem to have been completely extirpated. In Spain, where the faithlessness of the Romans often drove the people into rebellion, they had to maintain their power sword in hand. A great war broke out there in B.C. 181, which continued to rage till B.C. 179, when Tiberius Sempronius Gracchus concluded a peace on fair and honourable terms, which was long and gratefully remembered by the Spaniards.

Philip of Macedonia had indeed assisted the Romans in their war against Antiochus, but his hatred against them was as strong as ever. He died in B.C. 179, and his successor, *Perseus*, at once began to make preparations for a fresh conflict with Rome, for which his father had left him ample means. When the last war against Rome broke out, in B.C. 171, Perseus, in consequence of his unwillingness to part with his treasures, lost some of his valuable allies. Although, therefore, he had gained at first some small advantages, he was totally defeated in B.C. 168 in the great battle of *Pydna*, by Æmilius Paulus. The king, with his children, friends, and treasures, fell into the hands of the Romans, and had to adorn the triumph of his conqueror. Macedonia was now made tributary to Rome, and in order to break its strength, the country was divided into four districts independent of one another.

Shortly after the battle of Pydna, one thousand of the most distinguished Achæans, accused of having secretly supported Perseus, were sent to Italy to be tried. But instead of having an opportunity afforded them for clearing themselves of the charge, they were kept as hostages and prisoners in various towns of Italy. After spending seventeen years in this manner, and when their number was reduced to three hundred, they were permitted to return to their country, without any trial having taken place. The island of Rhodes, against which a similar charge was brought, lost its Asiatic possessions, and had to recognise the supremacy of Rome. In the year B.C. 149, Andriscus, a runaway slave, pretending to be a son of the late king Perseus, came forward claiming the throne of Macedonia. As just at that time a third war against Carthage was breaking out, the Macedonians, thinking it a favourable opportunity of recovering their independence, flocked round the standard of the pretender. But *Cæcilius Metellus* crushed him and his followers in a battle near Pydna, B.C. 148, and a few years later Macedonia was constituted as a Roman province.

While Metellus was still engaged in settling the affairs of Macedonia, the Romans sent an embassy to Greece calling upon the Achæans to dismiss Sparta and some other cities from their league. When the ambassadors communicated this order to the Achæans assembled at

Korinth, they were treated with insult, and there remained nothing but to compel the light-headed Greeks by force. In B.C. 147, Metellus, after having made the necessary arrangements in Macedonia, proceeded southward with his army, and defeated the Achæans in two battles. He himself, having a great affection for the Greeks, did all he could to prevent them engaging in a contest with Rome. But his term of office was coming to a close, and he was obliged to hand over the command of the army to the rude soldier *Lucius Mummius*, who, after defeating the Greeks in a battle on the Isthmus, took and destroyed the wealthy and splendid city of Korinth, B.C. 146. Its inhabitants were either put to the sword or sold as slaves, and the numerous treasures of art were wantonly destroyed or carried to Rome to adorn the villas and palaces of the aristocracy. But it was not only Korinth that suffered, for Mummius and his soldiery traversed Peloponnesus, spreading desolation everywhere. Under the oppressive rule of the Romans the prosperity of many once flourishing cities died away, and with it patriotism and the love of liberty gradually vanished. The Spartans continued to indulge their warlike propensities by selling their services to any foreign state that needed them, while the Athenians were valued by their conquerors chiefly as scholars, artists, poets, actors, or dancers, though they rarely gained their esteem and respect.

After the close of the Second Punic War, Carthage during a period of upwards of fifty years had to some extent recovered its former prosperity by industry, commerce, and agriculture. But as this prosperity increased, so also did the hatred and jealousy of Rome; and Masinissa, the neighbour of Carthage, at the instigation of the Romans, neglected no opportunity of harassing and annoying the reviving state. One Roman in particular, Cato, under the influence of a blind and infatuated hatred of Carthage, insisted in every speech he made in the senate upon the necessity of destroying Carthage. Masinissa, knowing that he might with impunity act towards Carthage in any manner he pleased, drove the unfortunate city into the necessity of defending its rights by force of arms. Upon this the Romans accused Carthage of having violated the peace. The Carthaginians, feeling the impossibility of successfully coping with Rome, assured the ambassadors that they had no hostile intentions, and not only sent three hundred of their noblest citizens as hostages to Rome, but offered to deliver up all their ships and arms. This happened in B.C. 149, and when all this was done, the Romans further demanded, that the Carthaginians should raze their own city to the ground and build a new one at a great distance from the sea. This insolent demand drove the people to madness and despair, and they resolved to perish amid the ruins of their own homes rather than yield to such flagrant insolence. All were seized with a bold patriotic spirit, and persons of all ranks and ages, women as well as men, cheerfully sacrificed all they possessed upon the altar of their country. The whole city was at once changed into a military camp, and nothing was spared that might serve to deliver the country from its impending doom. Such a spirit was too much even for the Roman legions, whose attacks upon the city were repeatedly repulsed. At last the Romans appointed *Cornelius Scipio Æmilianus*, a young man who had already given evidence of great military talent, to the consulship for the year B.C. 147. But even he was unable to overcome the desperate resistance of the Carthaginians, for although they suffered from the most terrible famine, they defended every inch of ground, even after the enemy had entered the city. The battle which raged in the streets lasted for six days, after which the fury of the invaders and a fearful conflagration changed the once proud mistress of the Mediterranean into a heap of ruins. Fifty thousand of its inhabitants who escaped from the massacre were sold as slaves; and Scipio, like his great namesake, was honoured with the surname of Africanus. The territory of Carthage was changed into a Roman province under the name of Africa, and a curse was pronounced upon the site of the ancient city, so that it should never be rebuilt.

Rome had now virtually become the mistress of all the countries around the Mediterranean, for the few states, such as Numidia, Egypt, and Pergamus, only enjoyed a nominal independence. But great as was the outward prosperity of the republic, at home matters were in a very different state, for while the upper classes had acquired the means of indulging in every kind of foreign luxury, a large class of Roman citizens was falling more and more into abject poverty. The political constitution of Rome had been finally settled long ago, the patricians and plebeians had long since been placed upon a footing of perfect equality; but a new aristocracy, called *nobiles* or *optimates* had gradually arisen, and though not recognised by law, based its claims upon wealth and family honours, that is, those who could boast of ancestors that had been invested with the great offices of the republic, looked upon themselves as entitled to the same honours, while those who had no such ancestors to boast of, were called obscure persons (*obscuri*); and if any such person succeeded in raising himself to any high office, which very rarely happened, he was stigmatised as an upstart (*novus homo*). The consequence of this was, that henceforth the struggle lay between the rich and the poor, that is, between those who possessed all the material and political powers, and those who possessed neither, but had to struggle hard to obtain the means of living.

Even before the conquest of Macedonia and Greece, the intellectual superiority of the latter had already shown its influence in all the departments of public and private life. Ever since the time of the Tarquins, Greek gods and Greek forms of worship had gradually found their way into Rome, and the ancient national religion had been so far forgotten, that its meaning and import were becoming matters of antiquarian speculation and research. The great Roman families thought it necessary to give their sons a Greek education, and make them conversant with the arts and literature of Greece. In fact the influence of the Greeks was so great, that Rome might have become a sort of corrupt Greek state, had the tendency not been checked by a body of men who still clung tenaciously to the ways and manners of their ancestors. This party was headed by *Porcius Cato*, who in his censorship did all he could to put down the prevailing fashion. In B.C. 155, he carried a decree by which three Greek philosophers, who had been sent to Rome as ambassadors and had attracted crowds of young men to their lectures, were ordered to quit the city. Long before this time, it had been found necessary to forbid the celebration of the festivals of Bacchus (*Bacchanalia*), which had been introduced into Rome from Southern Italy, and at which every kind of vice and licentiousness was practised. Cato counteracted the tendency of the age, not only by legal enactments but also by his writings on agriculture and on the early history of the Italians. But even he, unable to swim against the current, commenced the study of Greek in his old age.

The enormous wealth accumulated at Rome produced vast changes among the citizens of the republic. Their humble dwellings were exchanged for stately villas surrounded by parks, and filled with costly furniture and precious works of art, carried away from the conquered countries and cities. The Roman ladies especially indulged in extravagant luxury and dress, against which legal enactments were powerless. The ancient and frugal mode of life, and the pursuit of agriculture, were more and more abandoned, young men preferring military service abroad to the peaceful employments at home. The great mass of the soldiers liked best to serve under a commander who connived at every kind of licence, for which they rewarded him by their votes in the assembly, when he offered himself as a candidate for any of the high offices. The besetting sin of those times was the hunting after popularity, which the wealthy nobles endeavoured to gain by every means, however base, and more especially by amusing the people with splendid games and exhibitions, for which the Romans at all times entertained a passionate fondness. Such games were not, as in Greece, a stimulus to noble deeds, but consisted of the fights of gladiators in the circus, which fostered cruelty and a delight in bloodshed.

While the nobles lived in a style resembling that of princes, large classes spent their lives in poverty and distress, which were accompanied as usual by vices and crimes of every kind; yet these poor Romans looked upon themselves as the lords of the earth, and treated with contempt those foreigners whom war had reduced to slavery. The traffic in slaves was most lucrative, and those who might be employed as secretaries, readers, teachers, or domestic servants, often fetched enormous prices, while the rude and half-savage natives of Corsica and Sardinia were sold at a very low price. But although Rome was thus inwardly decaying very fast, its outward prosperity still continued to increase, and the great public works executed during this period, such as high roads, canals, aqueducts, and the like, sufficiently attest the grand and persevering energy of the Romans.

The nobles, for obvious reasons, were ever eager for fresh wars, and when appointed governors of foreign provinces, they were sure of being able to amass enormous wealth. The taxes to be paid by the provinces were not levied by the government itself, but were farmed by wealthy capitalists (*publicani*), who paid to the state a fixed sum, for which they obtained the right either themselves or through their agents to collect the taxes. Such a system opened a wide field for extortion and oppression. Whenever a country became a Roman province, it was immediately overrun by usurers and money-lenders, who soon absorbed what was left by the tax-gatherers. There existed, indeed, laws against extortion in the provinces, and their inhabitants might apply to the Roman senate for redress, but as the judges had either been guilty of similar offences or were looking forward to them as means of enriching themselves, the accused generally escaped with impunity.

But the misrule of the governors of provinces and the extortion of the publicani often drove the provincials into open rebellion. Such was the case in *Lusitania* in Spain, where *Sulpicius Galba* treacherously caused the people to assemble before him without their arms, and then let his soldiery loose upon them and had them all massacred. *Viriathus*, a brave Lusitanian, who had escaped on that terrible day, rallied round him as many of his countrymen as he could, and waged a desperate war against the Romans, which lasted from B.C. 148 to B.C. 140, and in which the Romans often suffered terrible reverses. In B.C. 141, the Romans were even obliged to conclude a peace with him, in which they had to recognise him as their friend and ally. This, however, was felt to be such a humiliation that in the year following the war was renewed; but even then they got rid of their enemy only by hiring assassins, who murdered him in his own tent. The Lusitanians indeed continued the war a few years longer, until in B.C. 137 they were compelled to submit.

Whilst the war against the Lusitanians was still going on, another broke out with the *Celtiberians*, B.C. 143. Their capital, *Numantia*, situated on a lofty eminence on the river Durius, was besieged for a period of five years, during which its inhabitants displayed the utmost bravery. In B.C. 137, the consul Hostilius Mancinus was reduced to such straits as to be obliged to conclude a peace with the Numantines, by which he had to recognise their independence. But the Roman senate refused to sanction the peace, and ordered Mancinus to be delivered up to the Numantines.

The war was thus renewed, and the Numantines, as before, defended themselves most heroically. Scipio, the destroyer of Carthage, then received the command of the army and the unenviable task of torturing to death a heroic people. He continued the siege with increased vigour, and the city suffered from such a terrible famine, that for some time they fed upon the corpses of their fellow-citizens, until at last in B.C. 133, after having killed their wives and children, they threw open the gates of their city and surrendered. The number of survivors was very small, and the long sufferings they had undergone had so much changed their features, that they scarcely resembled human beings. Scipio then destroyed the city, the ruins of which still exist, a monument of the brave struggle of the Numantines for freedom and independence. Spain now became a Roman province, and being completely exhausted, remained quiet for many years.

In the year in which Numantia fell, *Attalus*, king of Pergamus, died and bequeathed his treasures and his kingdom to the Roman people. Two years later, Aristonicus, a relative of the late king, disputed his will and claimed the kingdom as his lawful inheritance. As he was supported by many who hated the Roman dominion, he was enabled to place himself at the head of a general insurrection of the Ionians and Lydians. This led to a war with Rome, which, with varying success, was continued into the year B.C. 130, when it was brought to a close by Perperna, who took Aristonicus prisoner and carried him to Rome in triumph. In this war the Romans had been assisted by *Mithradates V.*, king of Pontus, who received as his reward the country called Phrygia, but the kingdom of Pergamus was constituted as a Roman province under the name of Asia.

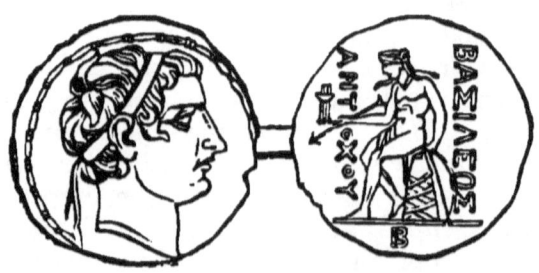

COIN OF ANTIOCHUS.

CAIUS MARIUS.

CHAPTER VIII.

FROM THE TIME OF THE GRACCHI DOWN TO THE FIRST WAR AGAINST MITHRADATES.

B.C. 133 TO B.C. 88.

THE Roman aristocracy, or the "optimates," as they called themselves, consisting of both patricians and plebeians, had gradually stepped into the place of the old patricians; and although the law did not recognise them as a distinct order, they nevertheless endeavoured by all means to secure the exclusive possession of the great offices and of the domain land. Their number was comparatively small, but they contrived to hold in their hands the administration of the republic and of the provinces, and thus they alone reaped wealth and glory from foreign wars. In this manner they amassed enormous riches, while multitudes were pining in poverty. The small landed proprietors who had once constituted the strength of the republic had nearly disappeared, and instead of them there had arisen a class of men who spent their life in idleness, and were ready to sell their votes to the highest bidder. Their number had latterly been much increased by the admission of freed men and strangers to the franchise. So long as the proprietors of large estates had them cultivated by free peasants or clients, things had gone on pretty fairly, but when the nobles began to employ bodies of slaves in their cultivation instead of free labourers, thousands of Roman citizens were reduced to the condition of beggars or vagrants. Many a wise and noble Roman seeing before him the abyss into which the republic was sinking, tried to devise remedies for the ever-increasing evil. In B.C. 139 the tribune *Gabinius* introduced the vote by ballot in the election of magistrates, and two years later the tribune *Cassius Longinus* carried a law introducing the same mode of voting in the popular law courts. But these measures, intended to prevent bribery, produced the opposite effect. A better remedy would have been to create an independent middle class by the distribution of the public land, of which the state possessed a vast amount, or to confer the franchise upon the Latins. The latter, however, was distasteful to the pride of the ruling people, and the former to the avarice and selfishness of the optimates. The fears entertained by far-sighted statesmen must have been greatly increased by the events which were just then happening in Sicily, where the slaves, headed by *Eunus*, in B.C. 134, broke out in open rebellion against their masters and the whole of the free population. This servile war, which lasted for upwards of two years, and was carried on with all the bitterness and ferocity of slaves bursting their chains, was brought to a close by Rupilius, and more than 20,000 slaves are said to have been killed in it.

Occurrences like these showed what might happen in Italy, if the actual system was persevered in. Many Romans saw the evil, but no one had the courage to come forward as a reformer, until in B.C. 133, *Tiberius Sempronius Gracchus,* a son of Cornelia, the daughter of the elder Scipio Africanus, after being elected tribune of the plebs, carried a law re-enacting the Licinian law, which, though it had never been repealed, had in the course of time become a dead letter. This law, as we have already seen, did not allow any person to hold more than 500 jugera of the public land; the surplus was to be taken from the actual possessors and distributed among poor citizens in small lots as their full property. A commission of three men was to be appointed to superintend the measurement and distribution. At the same time it was proposed that the property which had just then been bequeathed to the Roman people by King Attalus, should be divided among those who received land, in order to enable them to purchase stock and agricultural implements. The optimates, headed by *Scipio Nasica*, opposed the bill with all their might, and induced the tribune Octavius to put his veto on the proposal of his colleague. In this scheme they succeeded all the more easily, because Octavius himself possessed more of the public land than the law allowed. Gracchus left no means untried to persuade his colleague to give up his opposition, but without success. He was therefore forced either to abandon his patriotic scheme altogether, or to get rid of Octavius. He adopted the latter course, which, though unconstitutional, yet was justifiable on moral grounds. In a numerously-attended meeting of the people he proposed and carried the deposition of Octavius. This procedure gave his opponents a handle against him, and with some show of justice they declared that he was upsetting the constitution of the republic, and even spread the malicious report that he was aiming at making himself king of Rome. The people in their ignorance being easily misled, began to suspect the motives of Gracchus, and when he offered himself as a candidate for the tribuneship for the following year, it was evident that his popularity had been undermined, and the optimates, with their followers, created a tumult, in which Gracchus with three hundred of his friends was killed. This scene of bloodshed was followed by every kind of persecution of the friends of the tribune, in which the nobles revenged themselves for the fear they had suffered of being deprived of their illegal possessions.

Although the optimates had gained a complete victory, still the tribunes had become aware of their power and influence, and by their perseverance succeeded in the years which now followed to carry several popular enactments. The optimates had recourse to various contrivances for getting rid of the men whose opposition they most dreaded; but all their machinations did not prevent *Caius Sempronius Gracchus*, the younger and more talented brother of Tiberius, from offering himself as a candidate for the tribuneship for the year B.C. 123. He was elected, and at once proposed and carried a number of laws, the object of all being to weaken the power of the optimates, and to make provisions for the poorer classes. One of them was the re-enactment of his brother's agrarian law.

His course of legislation had made him so popular, that without much opposition he was re-elected tribune for the following year. His legislative activity was as great in the second as it had been in the first year. The first law he carried ordained that the law courts, which had hitherto been composed of senators only, should henceforth consist of equites or wealthy capitalists, so that, for example, senators accused of extortion in the provinces were no longer tried by their peers, but by a body of men believed to be honest and independent. Another law had reference to the distribution of the provinces, which henceforth was to take place before the election of the magistrates. Other measures were designed to give employment to the poorer classes in the making of public roads, constructing of public buildings, and other useful undertakings. His work proceeded as satisfactorily as could be expected; but when, urged on by his friend *Fulvius Flaccus*, he proposed that the franchise should be conferred upon the Latins, the optimates prevailed upon Livius Drusus, one of the tribunes, to outbid Gracchus in popular measures, and to promise the people other and greater advantages. By this means they succeeded in undermining the popularity of Gracchus, and in preventing his re-election to the tribuneship for the third year. When his second year of office had come to a close and he was divested of the sacred character of a tribune, his enemies gave the reins to their rage, and during the disturbances which then ensued, the consul Opimius, a personal enemy of Gracchus, was called upon by the senate to save the republic, as the cry was, from impending ruin. A regular battle was fought in the streets of Rome, in which Falvius Flaccus with three thousand of his followers were slain. Gracchus escaped across the river into the Grove of the Furies, where, by his own request, he was killed by a faithful slave. Executions and exile then completed the work which the sword had left undone, and the optimates, when satiated with blood, committed the blasphemy of erecting a temple to Concord. However, their triumph was not of long duration, and events were happening destined to bring their misdeeds into still more striking relief.

The measures of the Gracchi, and their immediate consequences form the beginning of a revolutionary period which terminated only with the downfall of the republic and the establishment of monarchy. The nobles had indeed gained the victory, but they made the worst possible use of it; they continued to indulge their insatiable avarice and the most barefaced bribery. But events were taking place destined to open the eyes of the Roman people to their disgraceful conduct. *Jugurtha*, the adopted son of Masinissa, knowing the venal character of the Romans, and feeling sure of impunity, if he could only lavish sufficient bribes upon the leading Romans, murdered the two sons of Masinissa, and made himself the sole ruler of Numidia. The Romans acted the part of mere lookers on, and were induced by large bribes to connive at the crimes of the usurper, until the tribune *Caius Memmius*, indignantly exposing the conduct of the nobles, prevailed upon the senate, in B.C. 111, to declare war against Jugurtha. The commanders of the army sent into Africa soon discovered that they could benefit themselves more by accepting the bribes of Jugurtha, than by adopting vigorous measures against him. When this became known at Rome, Memmius again fearlessly exposed the shameless conduct of those who had been entrusted with the management of the war. Jugurtha was then summoned to Rome, and even now might have escaped punishment, had he not had the audacity to murder young Massiva, a grandson of Masinissa. He was ordered to quit Rome, and the war was continued, but in so careless a manner, that the senate, alarmed at the growth of popular indignation, in B.C. 109, entrusted the command against Jugurtha to the proud, but brave and honest *Cæcilius Metellus,* who for a period of two years managed the war in a very creditable manner, and restored the honour of the Roman arms.

When he went to Africa, he took with him *Caius Marius* as one of his lieutenants. Marius was a man of humble origin, but of unbounded ambition and full of hatred of the aristocracy, whose polished manners he despised. He had already distinguished himself and gained much popularity by the vigorous manner in which he had opposed and attacked the proceedings of the nobles. His personal valour and military talents also were generally known, and the people even then seem to have looked upon him as the only man capable of bringing the war against Jugurtha to a close. The year after his arrival in Africa, he asked permission of his commander to go to Rome to offer himself as a candidate for the consulship. The insolent manner in which Metellus treated him on that occasion only fired his ambition. On his arrival at Rome he was received with the greatest enthusiasm by the popular party, and not only obtained the consulship for B.C. 107, but was commissioned to undertake the war against Jugurtha as the successor of Metellus. Marius, in organising his army, enlisted large numbers of the poorer classes, and even freed men, and trained them in so excellent a manner, that they became more than a match for the crafty Numidian, who was driven to such straits, that he applied to Bocchus, his father-in-law, for assistance. But *Cornelius Sulla,* a young noble, who was serving in the army of Marius as quæstor, induced Bocchus to deliver up Jugurtha, and Sulla brought him as a prisoner to Marius. This terminated the war, B.C. 106. Jugurtha was carried to Rome in triumph, and then thrown into a dungeon, where he was starved to death.

Italy was at this time threatened by an invasion of barbarians, more terrible than any it had yet experienced, and it was most fortunate that the Roman armies were no longer needed in Africa. The *Cimbri*, a Keltic host, pressed forward by commotions among eastern nations, appeared in Noricum in B.C. 113, where they were joined by another host of wandering *Teutones* or Germans. The Cimbri had no other object but to find new homes in Western Europe, and promised to commit no act of hostility against the Romans or their allies. They kept their promise, but being nevertheless treacherously attacked by the Romans near Noreia, they completely defeated them. They then proceeded into Gaul, which they ravaged in all directions; and in the course of four years several Roman armies were routed by the invaders on the banks of the Rhone and on the lake of Geneva. Rome was alarmed as in the days of Hannibal, and Marius again was the man to whom all looked with confidence. Although he had not yet returned from Africa, he was elected in his absence to the consulship for B.C. 104, and the same honour was conferred on him successively in the four following years. The Cimbri, after their several victories over the Romans, instead of invading Italy, proceeded to Spain, which they ravaged in the same manner as they had ravaged Gaul; but in B.C. 102 they returned to Gaul, where in the meantime the Teutones also had arrived.

Ever since his second consulship Marius had with great care trained and disciplined his army for the coming struggle, and when the Cimbri returned from Spain, Marius fought a great battle near Aquæ Sextiæ (Aix) against the Teutones, and their whole body was nearly annihilated. But meanwhile the Cimbri were descending from the Alps into Italy, and the army opposed to them under *Lutatius Catulus*, had to retreat before them to the southern bank of the Po. On hearing of this, Marius with his forces hastened to his relief, and at a place called Campi Raudii, near Vercellæ, he defeated, in B.C. 101, the Cimbri as completely as he had the year before defeated the Teutones. Marius was now universally greeted as the deliverer of Italy, and the sixth consulship, B.C. 100, was the reward of his glorious victories.

The popular or democratic party was now triumphant, and the nobles fearing to lose what they considered their rights, united under the leadership of Sulla, who was no less ambitious than Marius, and combined in his person all the vices and virtues of the Roman aristocracy. He had a special hatred of Marius, who, elated by his victories, acted in many ways as if he were the master of the Roman republic, and even supported the infamous tribune Appuleius Saturninus, who tyrannised over the assembly of the people, and by main force and violence carried a number of enactments, one of which proposed that the lands conquered by Marius in Africa and Gaul should be distributed among his veterans. Cæcilius Metellus, who opposed the revolutionary schemes of the tribune, was sent into exile. Saturninus succeeded in causing himself to be elected twice to the tribuneship by murdering his competitors in broad daylight. In B.C. 100 he went so far as to cause the murder of the high-minded Caius Memmius, because he wished to secure the consulship for his friend Servilius Glaucia. This, and many other atrocities, at length induced Marius openly to declare against Saturninus, and when he called upon the citizens to defend the republic, the people readily took up arms against the monster. Saturninus, with Glaucia and his followers, withdrew to the Capitol, where they were besieged; but want of water compelled them to surrender, and Marius ordered nearly all of them to be put to death. After these scenes, Marius for a time withdrew from public life, and the party feuds seemed to be subsiding.

But Sulla neglected no opportunity of wounding the feelings of Marius, especially by trying to show that the honour of having brought the war against Jugurtha to a close belonged to him, and not to Marius. But far weightier matters than these personal disputes were agitating the public mind. The reform introduced by

Gracchus regarding the courts of law had proved a complete failure, for the equites were found to be as accessible to bribes as the senators had been before, and in fact the one body helped and played into the hands of the other; the number of poor was increasing year by year, which enabled the rich by their bribery to monopolise all political power; and lastly, the Latins and Italian allies had become very clamorous in demanding the Roman franchise. Few men had the courage to grapple with these questions, but in B.C. 91, the eloquent tribune *Livius Drusus* undertook the task. His first attempt consisted in a proposal to divide the judicial power equally between the senators and the equites; he next aimed at checking the increase of pauperism, by distributing the public land among the poor and by the establishment of colonies; his third measure demanded the franchise for all the Italians. The exasperation of the nobles against him was so great, that before he was able to bring forward his third bill, he was murdered in his own house. The Italian allies, now seeing that it was useless to try to obtain what they wanted by constitutional means, resolved to conquer by force of arms what was so recklessly refused to their demands. A war thus broke out in B.C. 90, commonly called the *Marsian* or *Social War*, which blazed forth at once in all parts of Italy.

The Romans had never extended the franchise beyond the thirty-five tribes, which number was completed about the end of the First Punic War. The rights enjoyed by the Latins and Latin colonies approached nearest to the Roman franchise, and it was evident that they must be the first to obtain equal rights with the Romans. The Italians had set their last hope upon the efforts of Livius Drusus, and when they were disappointed in this, all the Sabellian nations, with the Marsians and Samnites at their head, formed themselves into a confederacy and declared their independence of Rome. Their plan was to establish an Italian republic governed by two consuls, and to make Corfinium, which was henceforth to be called Italica, its capital. The armies of the confederates were well trained, and the ample means for conducting the war seemed to promise success; but fortunately for Rome, the Latins throughout Italy as well as the Etruscans and Umbrians, did not join the confederacy, and in order to prevent their doing so, a law was proposed and carried at once, by Lucius Julius Cæsar, B.C. 90, whereby the franchise was conferred upon all the Latins; and two years later, when the Etruscans and Umbrians were on the point of joining the confederates, Rome wisely propitiated them also, by granting them the franchise. The war had in the meantime been carried on in several parts of Italy, and many a bloody battle had been fought. But the concessions made by Rome to the Latins, Etruscans, and Umbrians broke the strength and the hopes of the allies. At the same time, Rome was anxious to restore peace in Italy, because it was threatened by a war with Mithradates, king of Pontus. Pressed by this danger, the franchise was promised to all the Italians who should lay down their arms by a certain day. This measure produced the desired effect, and terminated the Social War, B.C. 88, in which Italy had lost 300,000 men. All accepted the offer except the Samnites, who afterwards joined Marius in his war against Sulla. The new citizens thus admitted to the franchise, were, however, not put on a complete footing of equality with the old ones, and, as we shall see hereafter, this arrangement gave rise to fresh civil disturbances.

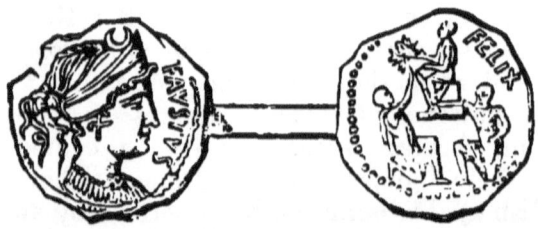

COIN OF SULLA.

A ROMAN ALTAR.

CHAPTER IX.

FROM THE FIRST WAR AGAINST MITHRADATES, DOWN TO THE DEATH OF SULLA.

B.C. 88 TO B.C. 78.

AT the time when the Romans were at war with Aristonicus, the claimant of the kingdom of Pergamus, they were supported, as we have seen, by Mithradates V., king of Pontus, for which they afterwards rewarded him by adding Phrygia to his kingdom. But as soon as Mithradates was dead, they took it away, and his successor, *Mithradates VI.*, being still very young and unable to resist the Romans at the time, strengthened himself by every means, especially by enlarging his kingdom. Mithradates had received a Greek education, and in addition to all the advantages which Greek culture could afford, he possessed great courage and enterprise. When he was sufficiently prepared to meet the Romans, he no longer hesitated to interfere in the affairs of countries allied with Rome; and his well-disciplined troops proved a match for the Romans whenever they met. As he advanced towards the west coast of Asia Minor, he was everywhere welcomed by the Greeks, who looked upon him as their deliverer from the Romans. In B.C. 88, he is said in one day to have ordered the massacre of 80,000 Romans residing in the different towns of Asia. When he had obtained possession of all Asia Minor, he sent his Greek general, *Archelaus*, with a large army into Greece, where his arrival was hailed by the chief cities, such as Athens and Thebes, as that of a deliverer.

These proceedings of the Pontian king called for immediate and energetic measures. The Roman senate accordingly entrusted the supreme command against him to *Sulla*, who was elected consul for B.C. 88. Sulla, who had distinguished himself in the Social War, was at the time still continuing the contest against the Samnites. Marius felt greatly hurt at being thus passed over, as the war against Mithradates was one in which glory and wealth would be the sure reward of the conqueror. Under the influence of this feeling, Marius allied himself with the tribune *Publius Sulpicius*, who, partly by violence and partly by a cunning distribution of the new citizens among the old thirty-five tribes, carried a proposal depriving Sulla of the command against Mithradates, and conferring it upon Marius. When Sulla was informed of this, he straightway marched with his army to Rome, which, being unprepared, was forced to admit him and his soldiers. The popular party offered a most determined resistance in the streets of the city, but Sulla succeeded in putting his enemies to flight. He used this victory with great moderation, outlawing only Marius and eleven of the most conspicuous leaders. Marius with great difficulty escaped to Minturnæ, and thence crossed over into Africa, where he is said to have spent his time among the ruins of Carthage, carefully watching the course of events in Italy.

Sulla spent some time at Rome, making such arrangements as might insure peace and tranquillity in the city during his absence in the East. He went so far in his moderation as to allow *Lucius Cornelius Cinna*, a leader of the democrats, to be elected consul for B.C. 87, together with his aristocratic friend, *Cneius Octavius*. Leaving the command against the Samnites to Pompeius Rufus, Sulla went with his army to Greece, where Thebes submitted to him without striking a blow. Archelaus, after two bloody battles, was put to flight. Sulla then marched against *Athens*, which, after a long siege, during which its inhabitants suffered from the most terrible famine, was taken and plundered, B.C. 86. His conduct towards Athens was marked by the greatest barbarity: the fortifications and even ancient temples were destroyed or pillaged, and a vast number of works of art was carried away. While these things were going on in Greece, Mithradates, being himself hard pressed in Asia by another Roman army under *Fimbria*, ordered Archelaus to negotiate for peace. The negotiations were protracted for a long time until B.C. 84, when Sulla himself went to Asia and had a personal interview with the king. Peace was then concluded on condition that Mithradates should pay all the expenses of the war, surrender his whole fleet, and give up all his conquests, so that his empire was limited to the original kingdom of Pontus. Sulla then proceeded to chastise the provinces and towns of Asia which had joined Mithradates, and exacted enormous fines from them, so that those countries for a long time after were in a state of complete exhaustion. Fimbria, though he had been very successful against the Pontian king, was treated by Sulla as an enemy, because he belonged to the party of Marius; and as he was deserted by his own soldiers, he put an end to his existence.

During Sulla's absence, Rome was again the scene of civil bloodshed, for Cinna attempted to abolish the regulations made by Sulla before his departure, and to recall the outlaws. But the party of the nobility in a fierce struggle drove him out of the city, and deprived him of the consulship. He then proceeded to the army engaged against the Samnites in Campania, where he assembled around him the malcontents from all parts of Italy, and invited Marius to return from Africa. Marius at once accepted the invitation, and after landing in Etruria, collected an army; in conjunction with Cinna, he marched upon Rome, which was compelled by famine and internal feuds to surrender. Marius now gave the reins to his desire for revenge upon his political opponents: bands of infuriated soldiers traversed the streets of Rome, murdering and robbing with impunity; and the leading aristocrats, such as Catulus, the consul Cneius Octavius, the orator Marcus Antonius, and many others, were slain, their houses plundered and destroyed, and their bodies left unheeded in the streets. For five days and five nights Rome suffered all the horrors of a city taken by the sword.

After these bloody proceedings, Marius caused himself to be elected to his seventh consulship for the year B.C. 86; but he did not long enjoy this honour, for he died about the middle of January. The war with the Samnites had in the meantime been brought to an end, and the franchise had been conferred upon them. All Italy was now completely in the hands of the popular party headed by Cinna, and the nobles urgently pressed upon Sulla to return home and save his party. But Sulla thought it right first to finish the work he had undertaken in Asia, and did not land in Italy till the beginning of B.C. 83. He proceeded at once to Campania; and as Cinna had been murdered by his own soldiers, the Marian party was deprived of the last able man among them, for those who now came forward as its leaders, such as Carbo, young Marius, and Norbanus, possessed neither the talent nor the energy required by the circumstances of the time. Sulla defeated them in several battles, and their soldiers came over to him. In B.C. 82, young Marius took refuge at Præneste, where he was closely besieged and driven to commit suicide. Sulla then entered Rome. At the same time, a Samnite army commanded by Pontius Telesinus, appeared before its gates, hoping to take the city by surprise; but Sulla met the enemy at the Colline Gate, where a most murderous battle was fought, in which the popular party was so completely defeated, that Pontius Telesinus in despair committed suicide.

By this battle Sulla became the undisputed master of Italy. All those who had to dread his vengeance took to flight, and a few days after the battle 8000 prisoners were butchered in the Circus, while the senate, assembled in the adjoining temple of Bellona, heard the cries and shrieks of the victims. Terrified by such scenes, the senate readily complied with all the commands of the conqueror. Although more than 100,000 lives had already been sacrificed during the civil war, Sulla, not yet satisfied, devised a new and unprecedented means for punishing those whom he suspected to have favoured his enemy. He set on foot a proscription, that is, a list of all those whom he chose to regard as his enemies was set up in public. Any one whose name was contained in that list might be killed, his estates were confiscated, and his descendants were for ever deprived of the franchise. This measure, though it was adopted under great provocation, is one of the most fearful recorded in history, for it tore asunder every tie of blood and friendship; sons betrayed their fathers, friends their friends, and slaves their masters, for it was a part of the proscription that those who protected or concealed a proscribed person, should be punished in the same way as the proscribed themselves. No less than 1600 equites were thus murdered, and among the monsters who distinguished themselves in those terrible days we find Catiline, of whom we shall hear more hereafter.

Having thus got rid of all his enemies, Sulla, in B.C. 82, caused himself to be appointed dictator for an indefinite period of time. And having by this means obtained unlimited power, he first of all rewarded those soldiers through whom he had risen to his present position, a proceeding quite new in Roman history. Twenty-three legions had colonies assigned to them, mainly in those towns which had supported his enemies. In these colonies, called *military* colonies, the soldiers constituted the ruling body, and being scattered all over Italy, they afforded the dictator a ready means of keeping the country in subjection. Moreover, 10,000 slaves were emancipated by him, and under the name of the Cornelii formed his bodyguard; and, lastly, he increased the number of senators by admitting into that august body a number of persons ready to do his bidding.

After these preliminary measures, the object of which was to secure his power, he proceeded to reform the constitution in a reactionary spirit. He first reduced the powers of the tribunes to what they had been originally, that is, the power to afford assistance against the arbitrary proceedings of a magistrate. By this means the comitia tributa were deprived of their legislative functions. His second measure restored to the senators the judicial power which Gracchus had assigned to the equites. Lastly, he increased the number of prætors to eight, that of the quæstors to twenty, and that of the pontiffs and augurs to fifteen. These and some other regulations respecting the administration of the provinces were his chief political reforms, and they show that he imagined the ancient spirit of the constitution could be restored by reviving its obsolete forms. Such reforms of course could not last. He was more successful in what he did for the criminal law, which he was the first to place on a solid and permanent basis.

After having made all these arrangements, Sulla, to the surprise of every one, in B.C. 78 laid down his dictatorship and withdrew to Puteoli, where he lived as a private person, and died the following year of a disease which had probably been brought on by his licentious mode of life. During his dictatorship, the scattered remnants of the Marian party had assembled in Sicily, Africa, and Spain, where their numbers were increased by malcontents. Pompey, who had greatly distinguished himself in the Social War, was despatched to Sicily and Africa, where he annihilated the opponents of Sulla by causing Carbo in Sicily to be assassinated, and by defeating Domitius Ahenobarbus in Africa. For this achievement, Pompey on his return obtained the honour of a triumph, although he was then only twenty-four years old.

During the same period, Rome was engaged in a second

war against *Mithradates*, which lasted from B.C. 83 to B.C. 81. The cause of it was that the Pontian king, after Sulla's departure, had repented of the peace, and as it had never been sanctioned by the Roman senate, he refused to give up Cappadocia, which he had promised to do. But he was betrayed by his general Archelaus, who persuaded Murena, the commander of the Roman forces in Asia, to attack the king at once, and not to wait until the king should take the offensive. Murena, acting on this advice, proceeded to Cappadocia, where he plundered the rich temple of Comana; but being attacked by Mithradates in the neighbourhood of Sinope, he was completely defeated. Peace, however, was then again concluded, B.C. 81, which left Mithradates in possession of at least a part of Cappadocia.

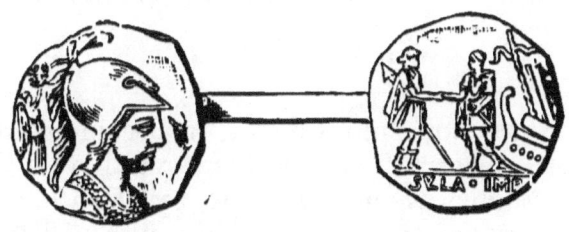

A MEDAL REPRESENTING THE MEETING OF SULLA AND MITHRADATES.

BUST OF POMPEY.

CHAPTER X.

FROM THE DEATH OF SULLA TO THE OUTBREAK OF THE WAR BETWEEN CÆSAR AND POMPEY.

B.C. 78 TO B.C. 49.

In the very year of Sulla's death, it became evident that his political reforms possessed no vitality. The first attempt to abolish them was made by *Æmilius Lepidus*, who failed because the party of Sulla was still too powerful. Similar attempts, however, were made year after year, until, in B.C. 70, Pompey, who himself had been a partisan of Sulla, carried a law by which the powers of the tribunes were restored to what they had been before the reform of Sulla; and in the same year *Aurelius Cotta* carried a bill by which the courts of law which Sulla had restored to the senators, were henceforth composed of senators, equites, and tribuni ærarii. Pompey in carrying and supporting these measures had no other object in view but to gain popularity, and this end he attained most completely, though more by good fortune than by any extraordinary abilities. He became the idol of the citizens as well as of the soldiers, and, in fact, the most popular man in Rome.

We have not yet mentioned what became of the remnants of the Marian party in Spain. In B.C. 82, when Sulla entered Rome, *Sertorius*, the best and ablest of the democratic leaders, having become disgusted with the reckless proceedings of his own party, went with a considerable force into Spain, in the hope of being able there to maintain the popular cause. He was soon joined by the exiled and persecuted followers of Marius, and by his prudence and military skill, he not only succeeded in attaching the soldiers to his person, but by his kindness he won the confidence of the Spaniards. His plan was to found an independent republic in Spain, in which Spaniards and Romans were to have equal rights. The new republic was to be governed by two consuls and a senate of three hundred members. A great public school also was established at Osca, in which the sons of Spaniards were to receive a Roman education. The plan at first succeeded admirably, and Sertorius enjoyed the confidence and affection of the Spaniards as well as of the Romans. War was commenced against him as early as B.C. 79, but neither Metellus nor Pompey was able to make any impression upon his excellently trained army. In B.C. 74, Sertorius entered into an alliance with Mithradates, whereby he hoped to place Rome between two fires. But disunion among the Spaniards saved Rome from this double danger. *Perperna*, one of the officers in Sertorius's army, whose ambition had been thwarted, in B.C. 72 formed a conspiracy against him, and caused him to be murdered at Osca during a banquet. Perperna then assumed the command of the army, but in his very first encounter with Pompey his whole army was routed, and he himself, having fallen into the hands of Pompey, was put to death. The Spanish republic thus came to an untimely end, and the Marian party was now utterly annihilated.

Ever since the Romans had become masters of the countries round the basin of the Mediterranean, the number of slaves both in Italy and in Sicily had been enormously increased. In the island a second servile war had been carried on from B.C. 102 to B.C. 99, in which thousands were killed on both sides. A similar but more dangerous insurrection broke out in B.C. 73 at

Capua, where about seventy slaves who were under training as gladiators, broke loose, and headed by the Thracian *Spartacus*, forced the prisons of other slaves in Southern Italy, and called on them to assert their freedom. Their number soon increased to ten thousand, all of whom were provided with arms. The object of these slaves seems to have been only to regain their liberty and to return to their homes; but having been successful against several consular armies, Spartacus formed the plan of attacking and destroying Rome itself. The free population of Southern Italy had been very much thinned during the Social War, and the slaves traversed the country murdering and destroying everything that came in their way. Fortunately for Rome, the slaves acted without any regular military organisation, and roamed over the country in irregular bodies. In consequence of this, *Licinius Crassus*, in B.C. 71, succeeded in gaining a complete victory over them; and as Spartacus himself fell in the battle, the slaves lost all hope of success. Thousands of them were captured and slain, and their bodies were impaled along the highroads, to strike terror into their fellow slaves; but a body of about five thousand escaped to the north of Italy, intending to proceed into Gaul. Just at this time Pompey, returning from Spain, fell in with them and completely cut them to pieces.

It was on his return from Spain to Rome, in B.C. 70, that he obtained the consulship, and for the sake of popularity assisted in abolishing the constitution of Sulla. After the expiration of his consulship, he lived for a time in private retirement, enjoying his popularity and waiting until a fresh opportunity for action offered itself. The same causes which had of late years increased the number of slaves, had also called into existence a number of pirates, infesting all parts of the Mediterranean, so that maritime commerce was exposed to the greatest dangers, and had almost become impossible. The pirates even plundered several coast towns, and ventured to destroy or capture ships at Ostia, the port town of Rome. They had their strongholds and warehouses chiefly in

Cilicia, on the south coast of Asia Minor. War had been waged against them ever since the year B.C. 78, but without any result, and Rome was in constant danger of famine. In these circumstances, the tribune *Aulus Gabinius*, in B.C. 67, proposed that Pompey should be invested for three years with the command in the Mediterranean and all its coasts, to a considerable distance from the sea; and that he should be amply provided with the means necessary to bring the war against the pirates to a close. Such a proposal might turn out dangerous to the very existence of the republic, and as such it was viewed by many; but the people did not hesitate to confer upon their favourite all that was demanded for him; and their confidence was fully justified, for the war which he now commenced and successfully terminated in about three months, was the most brilliant feat he ever accomplished. He completely swept with his fleet the Mediterranean, proceeding from west to east, and drove the pirates into the Cilician Sea, where he routed them in a great battle. The survivors were taken prisoners or surrendered; and Pompey, after destroying their strongholds, assigned to them settlements in which they might be able to gain their means of living without again resorting to piracy; for most of them can scarcely be called criminals; they chiefly consisted of people who had been impoverished and had become homeless by the Roman conquests in the East.

After having terminated this war in so brief a period, Pompey remained in Asia, probably in the hope of receiving the command in the third war against Mithradates, in which Rome had already been engaged for some years. The king of Pontus, as we have already noticed, had been tempted in B.C. 74, by Sertorius to renew his hostilities against Rome. It so happened that Nicomedes, king of Bithynia, had just died and bequeathed his kingdom to the Romans. Mithradates at once refused to recognise this bequest, and invaded Bithynia, while his fleet, after a naval victory over the Romans, laid siege to the wealthy town of Cyzicus, which was in alliance with

Rome. Meanwhile, *Lucullus*, who had arrived with his army in Asia, in B.C. 73, cut off the king from all supplies of provisions. This and some other losses sustained by Mithradates seemed to render his condition hopeless, and he fled to his son-in-law, Tigranes, king of Armenia, while Lucullus invaded Pontus, and compelled the towns to surrender one after another. Lucullus then set about regulating the affairs of the conquered countries; and when Tigranes refused to deliver up Mithradates, Lucullus, in B.C. 69, marched to Tigranocerta, the capital of Armenia, in the neighbourhood of which he defeated a vast army of Asiatics. Both kings then took to flight; but Tigranes, venturing upon another battle, was beaten a second time, near Artaxata; and Lucullus now thought of subduing the whole of Armenia, when a mutiny broke out among his soldiers, which was headed by *Publius Clodius*. Lucullus succeeded indeed in quelling the mutiny; but Mithradates, availing himself of the opportunity, returned to his kingdom, and Lucullus, though acting with energy, was prevented by the mutinous spirit of his army from gaining his end. Just at this time, B.C. 67, Lucullus had to give up the command to Acilius Glabrio, who had been sent from Rome as his successor. Glabrio, far from following in the footsteps of Lucullus, let all the advantages gained by his predecessor slip out of his hands, and Mithradates was enabled to regain possession of Pontus and Cappadocia. Lucullus, who had amassed enormous wealth, now returned to Italy, where his palaces and villas were always open to men of refined taste in art and literature. He is said to have introduced into Italy the cherry-tree from Cerasus, a town in Colchis; and the name cherry is therefore supposed to be derived from Cerasus.

What Pompey had expected was now coming to pass, for the ever-increasing power of Mithradates and the want of success of the Roman commander, afforded to the friends of Pompey a welcome opportunity of getting the command against Mithradates conferred upon him. Accordingly, in B.C. 66, the tribune *Manilius* brought forward a bill to this effect, which, being supported by some of the leading men, conferred upon him all the powers necessary to bring the war against the Pontian king to a close. Having received large reinforcements, Pompey attacked Mithradates on the banks of the Euphrates, where the king was utterly defeated and put to flight. Tigranes at the same time received back the sovereignty of Armenia at the hands of Pompey. Mithradates, who had fled into Colchis, was pursued by Pompey, who as conqueror traversed Albania and Iberia, countries about Mount Caucasus; but owing to the difficulties he encountered in those remote regions, he gave up the pursuit. While Mithradates was forming the bold plan of invading Italy from the north, in conjunction with Scythian tribes, an insurrection broke out among his own soldiers at Panticapæum, in the Crimea. The insurrection was headed by the king's own son, *Pharnaces;* and Mithradates, finding that his life was not safe, destroyed himself by poison, B.C. 63. When the body was sent to Pompey, he ordered it to be buried with regal magnificence; but nevertheless rewarded the unnatural son with the sovereignty of the country about the Cimmerian Bosporus.

Pompey then proceeded to Syria, and began to dispose of kingdoms as if he had been the sovereign of the world. Thus Antiochus, king of Syria, was deposed, and his kingdom, together with Phœnicia, was changed into a Roman province. Several countries in Asia Minor were given to kings ready to recognise the supremacy of Rome, while Bithynia, with a portion of Pontus, was made a Roman province. In Judæa, he displayed the same arbitrary proceedings, for having taken the Temple of Jerusalem, he appointed Hyrcanus tetrarch, while his brother Aristobulus, with his children, was carried to Rome as a prisoner.

When all these arrangements were made, Pompey, in B.C. 62, left Asia, but did not arrive in Rome till the beginning of the year following. He celebrated a most magnificent triumph, and immense sums of money amassed in Asia were handed over to the treasury of the republic. His popularity was so great that he might have done anything with impunity; but he affected great humility, making the people believe that he wished to be no more than a simple citizen. He was, however, most anxious to obtain from the senate the sanction of the arbitrary arrangements he had made in Asia, and he felt extremely hurt when he found that his wishes in this respect were opposed by men of the greatest influence; he was, in fact, so mortified, that he abandoned the cause of the optimates and joined the popular party.

Some time before Pompey's return, *Cicero* had saved the republic from a terrible conspiracy, headed by the infamous *Catiline*. Cicero was born at Arpinum in B.C. 106, and by his talent, industry, and irreproachable conduct, had so much distinguished himself, that, although he could not boast of great ancestors, he obtained the great offices of the state, one after another, as soon as he attained the age prescribed by law, and was raised to the consulship for the year B.C. 63. He was the greatest orator of the time, possessed great legal knowledge, and was the first Roman who popularised the philosophical speculations of the Greeks among his countrymen. As a statesman he was often led into inconsistencies and contradictions, partly owing to his friendship for both Cæsar and Pompey. He has often been blamed for his vanity, of which perhaps he cannot be acquitted, though much may be said to excuse it. In Cicero's consulship, Catiline, a patrician of a most profligate character, and overwhelmed with debts, formed a conspiracy which was joined by many reckless nobles, whose circumstances, like those of Catiline himself, were so desperate that they saw no hope of saving themselves except by a revolution. Catiline had attempted similar things before, but had been defeated by the watchfulness of the authorities and by his own impatience. He now determined to murder Cicero, to set fire to the city of Rome, to overthrow the constitution, and in the midst of the confusion to usurp the reins of government; but the vigilance of Cicero prevented the infamous scheme. Catiline's secret proceedings were brought to light by the consul, and he himself quitted the city and joined an army of conspirators already assembled at Fæsulæ. The senate, on the proposal of Cicero and Cato, condemned him and some of his associates who had remained at Rome to death. The latter were strangled in prison, but Catiline himself and the army of Fæsulæ were defeated in a furious battle near Pistoria, in the north of Etruria. Cicero was overjoyed at having saved his country; but his happiness did not last long, for many of the friends and secret supporters of Catiline still remained at Rome, eagerly watching for an opportunity of taking vengeance upon him.

We have already seen that, ever since the time of Marius and Sulla, the leading object of the men in power was to gain popularity at any cost, and that not with a view to benefit their country, but to gratify their own ambition and avarice. Hence the history of this period, down to the establishment of the monarchy, is little more than the personal history of men who endeavoured to outdo one another. By far the most eminent and most talented among them was *Caius Julius Cæsar*, born in B.C. 100, and belonging to one of the most ancient patrician families. He was fast rising in popular favour at the time when Pompey was quietly enjoying the fruits of his victories. Cæsar was a man of the highest culture, and indefatigable in all he undertook, but unscrupulous in regard to the means he employed to gain his end. He was equally great as an orator, an author, a general, and a statesman. An aunt of his had been married to Marius, for whom he always entertained great affection; and in B.C. 65 he openly came forward as the leader of the popular party. His liberality was unbounded, whence he became overwhelmed with debts; but a campaign against the revolted Lusitanians, B.C. 61, enabled him to acquire sufficient wealth to satisfy his creditors, as well as his own extravagant wants. In B.C. 59 he obtained the consulship; he strengthened himself by a close alliance with Pompey, and by effecting a reconciliation between Pompey and Crassus. These three men came to an agreement, that no political measures should be allowed to be passed, unless they were agreeable to all three. They thus held the fate of the republic in their hands, and a number of popular measures were adopted, among them an agrarian law, by which 20,000 citizens received assignments of public land. Cæsar at last also prevailed upon the senate to sanction Pompey's arrangements in Asia, and caused Cisalpine and Transalpine Gaul, together with Illyricum, to be assigned to himself as his provinces, which he was to administer after the expiration of his consulship.

Cæsar, however, did not at once proceed to his provinces, but remained in the neighbourhood of Rome until the end of April B.C. 58. The object of this seems to have been to support *Clodius*, who bore a grudge against Cicero, and by the aid of Cæsar obtained the tribuneship for B.C. 58. After having ingratiated himself by several popular measures, he carried a law whereby every one was declared an outlaw who had put to death a Roman citizen without a formal trial. This was aimed at Cicero, who on the mere authority of the senate had caused some of the associates of Catiline to be strangled in prison. Cicero, knowing this, went into exile in order to escape condemnation. He was then formally declared an outlaw, his house in the city was burnt, and two of his villas were destroyed. But no sooner had Clodius's tribuneship expired, than a reaction took place in public feeling, in consequence of which Cicero, being recalled from exile in B.C. 57, returned to Rome amid the greatest rejoicings of the people.

While Cæsar was engaged in Gaul, the administration of which had been assigned to him for five years, things in Rome did not go very smoothly. In B.C. 55, when *Pompey* and *Crassus* were consuls, a law was carried by which Cæsar's government of Gaul was prolonged for other five years, while Pompey obtained Spain, and Crassus Syria, for the same period. Pompey, exercising a sort of dictatorial power, remained at Rome, leaving the administration of Spain to his lieutenants; but Crassus, tempted by the rich province of Syria, proceeded thither with his army, robbing and plundering wherever he appeared; and in B.C. 54 undertook an expedition against the *Parthians*, who had formed a powerful empire on the east of the Euphrates; but after having crossed the river he was utterly defeated in a battle near Carrhæ, taken prisoner, and killed, together with his son. The Roman army was nearly annihilated, and the camp and all the standards fell into the hands of the conquerors.

When Cæsar arrived in Transalpine Gaul, only its southern part, the country about the mouths of the Rhone, had been conquered and constituted as a province; but Cæsar was determined to conquer the whole country, for which its invasion by the Germans and a migration of the Helvetii afforded a welcome pretext. In this he succeeded completely. He was even tempted to invade Germany, though probably for no other object than to strike terror into the natives. In the summer of B.C. 55 he undertook an expedition into Britain, because its inhabitants had supported the Gauls against him, and because he was invited by a British prince who had been deprived of his throne by a usurper. The Britons offered a vigorous resistance, and although he gained a victory over them, he was compelled by the late season of the year to return to Gaul. In the following year he invaded the island a second time, and advanced to the north of the Thames, conquering the greater part of Essex and Middlesex. After having defeated the natives several times, he concluded peace with them, on condition that they should pay an annual tribute and give hostages. Cæsar then returned to Gaul; but as he was unable to leave behind any troops to keep the conquered part in subjection, the promises of the Britons were soon forgotten or neglected. The war in Gaul was then continued with great vigour, and not without great difficulties and losses.

In B.C. 50 Cæsar returned to Cisalpine Gaul, leaving the greater part of his army in Transalpine Gaul. The men who had served under him for so many years were attached to him in the highest degree, and his extraordinary exploits had everywhere created the greatest admiration of his genius and skill.

In the meantime Pompey had neglected nothing to increase his popularity. After the fall of Crassus, the Roman republic was virtually governed by Cæsar and Pompey. The former, during his wars in Gaul, had kept up an active correspondence with his friends at Rome; and his partisans, *Clodius, Curio*, and others, received enormous bribes from him. Their proceedings had sometimes been of a most turbulent and violent kind. The Roman aristocracy, alarmed at the increasing influence of Cæsar, again began to look upon Pompey as the man who alone could save them from the machinations of the popular party. In B.C. 51, *Claudius Marcellus*, one of the principal nobles, proposed that Cæsar should be recalled and a successor appointed; no opportunity was, in fact, overlooked, for hurting or insulting him. The time seemed at last to have come when the optimates thought it necessary to resort to energetic measures; and the senate passed a decree, peremptorily demanding of Cæsar to disband his army by a certain day, and declaring him a public enemy if he should refuse to do so. Two tribunes had in vain opposed the decree, and demanded that Pompey should likewise resign his power and disband his armies; but not being listened to, and pretending that their lives were not safe, they fled to Cæsar, who was stationed at Ravenna, with only a small part of his forces, and called upon him to proceed to Rome as the avenger of the tribunician power. Pompey and the optimates had the fullest confidence in their resources, and even the most necessary precautions were neglected.

VESTAL VIRGIN.

BUST OF JULIUS CÆSAR.

CHAPTER XI.

FROM THE CIVIL WAR BETWEEN POMPEY AND CÆSAR, DOWN TO THE BATTLE OF ACTIUM.

B.C. 49 TO B.C. 31.

THE fugitive tribunes found Cæsar at Ravenna. Having heard the report of what was going on at Rome, he hesitated for a moment, as to whether he should cross the Rubicon, a little stream which separated his province from Italy. When he had made up his mind, he called out, "The die is cast," and having sent orders for the legions in Gaul to follow him, he crossed the river with his small force. Accompanied by his veterans, who were devoted to him, he hastened southward, hoping to surprise his enemies before they had completed their preparations; and all the towns on his route readily opened their gates to him. Pompey, who was roused too late from his feeling of security, had not the courage to await the arrival of his opponent at Rome; but with only a few trustworthy soldiers, an army of hastily-levied and untrained recruits, and accompanied by a large number of the optimates, he fled to Brundisium, and on the approach of Cæsar crossed the Adriatic with his followers. He must now have seen the folly of his belief, that he only needed to stamp the ground with his foot to call forth legions. Cæsar, not having a fleet at his command, returned to Rome. All Italy joined him, and he displayed extraordinary kindness and affability, though he acted as if he had been the sovereign of the republic. He took possession of the treasury, and leaving Pompey to his fate, at once proceeded to Spain against Afranius and Petreius, the lieutenants of Pompey. By his astonishing rapidity and military skill, he compelled them, in a battle near Ilerda, to surrender. The commanders were dismissed unhurt, and the army was disbanded. On his return he had to force Massilia, which desired to remain neutral; and the city, though taken, was treated with great mildness. Meanwhile, Cæsar's friend Curio, who had been sent into Sicily, took possession of the island; but having crossed into Africa for the purpose of driving out the friends of Pompey, he was killed by Juba, king of Numidia.

While yet engaged in reducing Massilia, Cæsar was appointed dictator, and in this capacity he returned to Rome; but in order not to hurt the feelings of the republicans too much, he caused himself to be elected consul for the year B.C. 48, and laid down the dictatorship. He hastily passed several measures to secure order and tranquillity in the city, restored the exiles and the children of those who had been proscribed by Sulla, conferred the franchise upon the inhabitants of Cisalpine Gaul, and took some other measures of an urgent nature. As soon as these necessary arrangements were completed, he sailed across the Adriatic in pursuit of Pompey, who had in the meantime gathered troops, ships, and supplies of every kind from all parts of the East, so that in point of numbers he was greatly superior to his adversary. Cæsar besieged **Pompey at Dyrrhachium**, but with so little success that he had to raise the siege. However, instead of despairing, he boldly marched across the mountains into Thessaly, and Pompey, imagining that he had taken to flight, followed him in all haste, in the hope of putting an end to the war by a single blow. Cæsar had pitched his camp near *Pharsalus*, and Pompey, urged on by his inexperienced and presumptuous followers, fought the famous battle in which his army was completely defeated. His camp, filled with every kind of luxury, fell into the hands of the conquerors. Pompey himself, seized with despair, fled to Egypt, where he had some reason to expect a kindly reception; but the king of Egypt, hoping to secure the favour of Cæsar, ordered him to be murdered, even before he reached the shore, and his body was left unburied on the beach.

A few days later, Cæsar, with a small force, arrived in Egypt, and the sad end of his rival is said to have brought tears into his eyes. The Egyptian king, however, did not receive the expected reward; for Cæsar, being called upon to act as mediator between him and his sister, *Cleopatra*, decided in favour of the beautiful and fascinating Cleopatra. This decision involved him in a war with the people of *Alexandria*, during which he, with his small force, was exposed to the greatest danger. But he defended himself in the royal palace with wonderful skill against the infuriated populace, and when the palace was set on fire, he only escaped by swimming to a ship anchored near the coast. Reinforcements, however, having arrived, Alexandria was compelled to surrender, and as the king had been drowned in the Nile during the disturbances, Cleopatra was now the recognised queen of Egypt, and Cæsar remained at her court for nine months, during which he appears to have forgotten everything in the luxuries of her court. But when at last he was informed that Pharnaces, the son of Mithradates, in his attempt to extend his kingdom, had defeated a Roman legate, Cæsar, in the spring of B.C. 47, marched into Pontus, and defeated Pharnaces in a decisive battle near Zela. This victory is famous for the laconic despatch which Cæsar sent to Rome about it—" I came, saw, conquered."

In the autumn of B.C. 47, Cæsar hastened back to Rome, where he was received with the greatest enthusiasm by the senate and people, and so many honours and powers were showered upon him that in point of fact he was made the sovereign of the republic, which was in a great measure the result of his mildness and clemency towards his former opponents. The remnants of Pompey's party had in the meantime gathered their scattered forces in Africa, where they were supported by King Juba. Cæsar, anxious to bring the war against them to a close, stayed only a short time at Rome, to reward his friends by increasing the number of prætors, quæstors, ædiles, and of the members of the priestly colleges. When these and certain conciliatory measures were settled, he proceeded to Africa, where the bloody battle of *Thapsus*, in B.C. 46, decided the fate of the Pompeian party for a time. Fifty thousand dead are said to have covered the field of battle, and many of the survivors put an end to their own lives. Among these latter were *Metellus Scipio*, Pompey's father-in-law; King *Juba*, *Petreius*, and *Cato*, who bled himself to death at Utica, because he could not bear the idea of living in a state which had lost its freedom. *Cneius* and *Sextus*, the two sons of Pompey, escaped into Spain, where afterwards they renewed the war.

Cæsar was now virtually the sole ruler of the Roman empire, and on his return from Africa he silenced all fears and apprehensions by proclaiming a general amnesty, and by assuring his fellow-citizens that his sole object was to restore peace and order. He celebrated four triumphs, and entertained both soldiers and citizens with every kind of public amusement. During his stay at Rome, in B.C. 46, he introduced his celebrated reform of the calendar, which, through the ignorance or caprice of the pontiffs, had fallen into the greatest disorder. Cæsar not only remedied the existing evil, but made regulations to prevent its recurrence; and the calendar, as reformed by him, remained in use until A.D. 1582, when Pope Gregory XIII. introduced another reformed calendar, which is still in use. While Cæsar was thus engaged in Rome, news was brought to him that the sons of Pompey had collected an army in Spain, and that the south of that country was in a state of insurrection. Accordingly, towards the end of B.C. 46, he set out for Spain, where he had to contend with almost insurmountable difficulties; but his undaunted courage and perseverance overcame them all, and the terrible battle of *Munda*, early in B.C. 45, decided the fate of the Pompeian party for ever. Cneius Pompeius was killed, but Sextus escaped, and for some years led the life of chief of robbers and pirates.

On his return to Rome, Cæsar celebrated another triumph, and was received by the senate with abject flattery and servility. Honours of every kind were showered upon him: he was called "the father of his country;" the month of Quintilis, in which he was born, was called after him Julius (July); the powers which he had received in the course of time were now granted to him for life; he received the permanent title of imperator, the consulship for the next ten years, and the dictatorship for life. These and other powers made him in point of fact the sovereign of the Roman empire, and nothing was wanting but the outward signs of sovereignty. He did indeed observe the ancient republican forms, to allay the fears of the republicans; he allayed the fears of the nobles by increasing the number of senators; he satisfied the soldiers by the distribution of land; he improved the laws and their administration; raised commerce and agriculture; embellished the city with temples and theatres; and benefited all Italy by making roads, canals, and harbours. But with all this he could not overcome the fears of the people, who perceived that he was not satisfied with the substance of sovereign power, but was aiming also at the outward marks and distinctions of a sovereign. The increasing pride of the dictator, and his obvious desire to assume the title of king, at length induced the republicans to make common cause with his personal enemies. A conspiracy accordingly was formed against his life, early in B.C. 44. It was headed by Junius Brutus, a genuine republican, and by Cassius, who bore a personal grudge against

Cæsar. Both had been raised by him to the prætorship and been treated with kindness and confidence, although they had been partisans of Pompey. The plan for murdering Cæsar was formed with the greatest caution and secrecy. He had summoned a meeting of the senate for the 15th of March B.C. 44, at which he was to receive the title of King out of Italy, for the purpose of carrying on a war against the Parthians. When on that day he arrived in the senate, the conspirators rushed upon him with their daggers. At first he attempted to defend himself, but perceiving Brutus among them, he exclaimed, "You too, Brutus?" wrapped himself up in his toga, and sank at the base of Pompey's statue. Thus fell the only man that was then both able and willing to save Rome from civil war, and whose reign might have been the beginning of a tranquil and prosperous era in Roman history.

The conspirators had acted in the belief that their deed would be looked upon as patriotic, and applauded by the whole population; but the little enthusiasm which it created was soon followed by hatred and detestation when Cæsar's friend Antony delivered the funeral oration, in which he set forth in glowing colours the great merits of the dictator, and the liberal gifts which in his will he had bestowed upon the people. The murderers, therefore, to save their own lives, had to quit Rome. Brutus and Cassius went to the East, where provinces had previously been assigned to them; and Decimus Brutus to Cisalpine Gaul, where he took up his position at *Mutina*. Antony, who caused Cisalpine Gaul to be assigned to himself as his province, at once proceeded to Mutina with an army to expel Decimus Brutus. Cicero during that time delivered several speeches against Antony, in consequence of which the senate invested *Julius Cæsar Octavianus*, the adopted son and heir of Cæsar, with the powers of prætor. Octavianus was then only nineteen years old, and, notwithstanding the warnings of his friends, had come to Rome from Apollonia, where he had been studying. Antony had in the meantime been declared a public enemy, and many of his veteran troops joined Octavianus, who, along with Hirtius and Pansa, the consuls of B.C. 43, proceeded to the north against Antony. Antony, after being defeated, fled into Transalpine Gaul, where he was kindly received by the governor Lepidus. The two consuls having fallen in the war of Mutina, the senate entrusted the command of the armies to Decimus Brutus; and Octavianus, enraged at what he considered a slight to himself as well as an insult to the memory of Cæsar, compelled the senate to allow him, notwithstanding his youth, to be elected to the consulship. A law was then passed, declaring the murderers of Cæsar outlaws, and Octavianus again marched to the north. Decimus Brutus took to flight, and was afterwards murdered at Aquileia; but Lepidus and Antony, being exempted from the decree of outlawry, returned to Italy.

Octavianus, Antony, and *Lepidus* then met together and assumed the title of triumvirs for regulating the affairs of the state, and distributed the provinces among themselves. Antony and Octavianus, moreover, undertook to carry on the war against Brutus and Cassius in the East. The triumvirs then, without having the excuse of Sulla, imitated his example by drawing up a proscription list, in which each of them entered the names of any persons whom he wished to get rid of. This measure was ostensibly directed against their political opponents, but in many cases persons found themselves among the proscribed, solely on account of their wealth, which the triumvirs coveted. The three then entered Rome with their armies, forced the people to sanction their arrangements, and then let loose their soldiers upon the unarmed citizens. The most illustrious and patriotic men fell under the strokes of the rapacious soldiery, and murder was the order of the day. Two thousand equites and three hundred senators were massacred, and those who could escape fled to Brutus and Cassius, or to Sextus Pompeius, who had in the meantime made himself master of Sicily. Cicero, who had praised Octavianus as the champion of liberty, and had supported him on all occasions, was one of the many victims; for in order to please Antony, Octavianus had allowed the name of the great orator to be put on the proscription list, and he was murdered on the 7th of December B.C. 43. His head was taken to Fulvia, the wife of Antony, who feasted her eyes on the dead features of the man who had so unmercifully attacked her husband's reckless and lawless proceedings.

When the triumvirs had wreaked their vengeance upon unhappy Italy by murders and confiscations, Octavianus and Antony sailed to the East to conduct the war against Brutus and Cassius.

Brutus was in his province of Macedonia, where he was recognised as the lawful governor, and had amply provided himself with everything necessary to meet his enemies. Cassius had been very active in Asia Minor and Syria; and the two republican chiefs, who were masters of nearly all the countries east of the Adriatic, met at Sardes, where they agreed upon their plans of operation. But while they were making preparations, Octavianus and Antony had already subdued Greece, and taken up their quarters at Amphipolis. The republicans pitched their camp in the neighbourhood of *Philippi*, and in the first engagement Cassius was forced to retreat before Antony, while Brutus repelled the legions of Octavianus, who himself took no part in the battle, on the ground of ill health. Soon after, Cassius, misled by false information and despairing of success, threw himself upon his own sword. Twenty days after the first battle, the triumvirs renewed the contest, in which Brutus, being defeated likewise, put an end to his life. His example was followed by many other republicans, and the rest of their soldiers partly surrendered and partly fled to Sextus Pompeius in Sicily. The battles of Philippi, in the autumn of B.C. 42, finally annihilated the republican party.

The conquerors now made a fresh division of the empire, in which Lepidus obtained Africa, and Antony the eastern provinces, while Octavianus received Italy, where he satisfied his soldiers by the distribution of land, and the establishment of military colonies on the model of those founded by Sulla. Antony, intoxicated by the flatteries of the Greeks and the luxuries of Asia, entered upon a voluptuous career, bordering upon insanity; and the sums he extorted in Asia were lavished upon Cleopatra, queen of Egypt. His wife *Fulvia*, who loved him most passionately, did everything she could to induce him to return to her. The establishment of the military colonies had thrown thousands of Italians into poverty, and this afforded to Fulvia and her brother-in-law *Lucius Antonius*, a fair pretext to come forward as the protectors of the poor and distressed. Lucius Antonius was consul in B.C. 41, and, together with Fulvia and others, took up a position at *Perusia*, in Etruria, where he proclaimed himself the friend and protector of the poor, and where large numbers flocked to his standards. Towards the end of the year, Octavianus, with three armies, commenced operations against them as rebels, and besieged them at Perusia. When the place began to suffer from famine, Lucius Antonius capitulated, and Fulvia was set free on condition that she should quit Italy. All the senators of Perusia, however, were put to death; and more than three hundred of its citizens were sacrificed, on the 15th of March B.C. 40, to Julius Cæsar. The town of Perusia was reduced to ashes, and Fulvia went to Greece, where she died soon after.

During the war of Perusia, hostilities were on the point of breaking out between Antony and Octavianus, and the former actually sailed with his fleet to Brundisium, and prevailed on Sextus Pompeius to join him; but a reconciliation was brought about, and Sextus Pompeius was declared the common enemy of the triumvirs. Pompeius now returned to his piratical practices, and prevented supplies from abroad being conveyed to Rome, in consequence of which the citizens began to suffer from famine. The people loudly complained, and demanded of the triumvirs to come to some arrangement with him. A peace was therefore concluded with him in B.C. 39, in which he was recognised as the governor of Sicily. Antony now married Octavia, the noble-minded sister of Octavianus, and proceeded to Greece, where for a time he lived as a private person. Pompeius, who justly considered himself wronged by Antony, not altogether abstaining from piracy, afforded Octavianus a fair pretext for undertaking a war against him. It was commenced in B.C. 38, but with no great success, until, in B.C. 36, Octavianus entrusted the command of the fleet to his friend *Agrippa*, who was supported by the fleets of Antony and Lepidus. But even now no impression was made on Pompeius, until he was defeated in the great battle of Mylae. His land army surrendered to the conquerors, but he himself fled into Asia, where soon after he was murdered. Lepidus, who appears to have been a man of no great talent or energy, was sent to Rome, where he lived as pontifex maximus until B.C. 12.

The Roman empire was now in the hands of Antony and Octavianus. In the year B.C. 40 a war had broken out with the Parthians, who had invaded Syria. The war was at first conducted very successfully by Antony's lieutenants, but in B.C. 37 Antony himself hastened to Syria to undertake the command in person. Although he had a large army, and was supported by the king of Armenia, the Parthian king Phraates, attacking him in Media, nearly annihilated his legions, and gained possession of all his ammunition and provisions. Antony himself escaped and returned to Alexandria in Egypt, where he forgot himself and everything else in the pleasures of the court. He not only gave to Cleopatra several provinces of the empire, but went so far as to celebrate a triumph at Alexandria, and to divorce his wife Octavia. Octavianus felt himself insulted in the person of his sister, and the Romans generally began to feel ashamed of Antony's conduct. At length, in B.C. 32, war was declared against the queen of Egypt; and early in the following year the fleet of Octavianus, commanded by Agrippa, appeared in the Adriatic, while Octavianus, with his army, landed in Epirus.

Antony, accompanied by Cleopatra, assembled his forces at Corcyra; and on the 2d of September B.C. 31, the memorable sea fight off the promontory of *Actium*, in Acarnania, commenced. Its issue was at first doubtful; but Cleopatra, losing hope, took to flight; and Antony, following her, proceeded to Alexandria, leaving his fleet and army to their fate. The fleet was soon destroyed by Agrippa; and the land army, finding itself abandoned by its commander, surrendered to Octavianus. The moderation displayed by Octavianus towards his vanquished enemies excited general admiration. Soon after his victory, in commemoration of which the town of Nicopolis was founded opposite Actium, he followed the fugitives to Alexandria. Cleopatra, on his arrival, tried to charm him as she had charmed Cæsar and Antony. But she did not succeed; and Antony being prematurely informed of her death, killed himself, B.C. 30; and Cleopatra soon after put an end to her existence, it is said, by putting a viper to her breast. By her death the race of the Ptolemys became extinct, and Egypt was made a Roman province. In the spring of B.C. 39, Octavianus returned to Rome, where the Temple of Janus was closed, a sign that peace was restored throughout the Roman empire, of which Octavianus was now the undisputed master.

MARCUS BRUTUS.

THE EMPEROR AUGUSTUS.

CHAPTER XII.

THE REIGN OF AUGUSTUS.

B.C. 31 TO A.D. 14.

THE revolutionary period was now closed; and after the fearful scenes through which Rome had passed ever since the time of the Gracchi, it was a real blessing for the empire now to be governed by a ruler really desirous to restore peace, order, and prosperity to his country. The thinking part of the Roman population must have arrived at the conviction that a republican government had become an impossibility. But Octavianus was nevertheless very careful to preserve the republican forms, such as the meetings of the popular assembly and of the senate; he also avoided giving offence by assuming the title of king or dictator, so that, notwithstanding his extraordinary powers, he was apparently only a republican magistrate. The great mass of unthinking Romans cared neither for republic nor monarchy, and were satisfied if well provided with bread and amusements.

When Octavianus, in B.C. 39, returned from the East, the senate and the people vied with each other in their servility and adulation. Two years later he received the title of *Augustus*, that is, the Venerable, a title which was afterwards assumed by all the Roman emperors. To the title of Augustus was added that of Imperator (emperor) for ten years, which, however, was afterwards renewed from time to time; and by it he obtained the supreme command of all the forces of the empire. In B.C. 23 he received the powers of a tribune for life, whereby his person became sacred and inviolate, and obtained the right to convene the senate whenever he pleased, and to put his veto upon any of its decrees. In this manner he acquired in a few years all the powers which had hitherto belonged to the several republican magistrates, though the consulship and the other high offices were as usual nominally conferred upon others, and continued to be looked upon as high distinctions coveted by the first men of the state. In his capacity of censor, Augustus directed his attention first to the clearing of the senate of unworthy members, and limited their number to 600. In the course of time, however, the senate became a sort of state council and supreme court of justice, which had to try all offences against the majesty of the emperor. He was supported in his administration of the empire by a number of able men, such as Agrippa, Maecenas, Valerius Messalla, and Asinius Pollio.

Augustus bestowed especial care upon the better administration of the city, where hitherto life and property had been anything but safe. In order to have complete control over the city as well as Italy, he distributed the former into fourteen regions, and the latter into a number of districts or provinces. For his own safety he established a body-guard of ten cohorts, three of which were stationed in the city, and the remaining seven in different parts of Italy; but in the reign of his successor Tiberius, they were all collected in a fortified camp close to the city. In regard to the provinces, the administration of which he greatly improved, he made an arrangement, in B.C. 27, by which some were assigned to the senate, and some to himself, reserving for himself those which still required the presence of a military force. The governors of the senatorial provinces were appointed by the senate, while the emperor nominated those of the provinces reserved to himself. The revenues of the senatorial provinces went into the state treasury, but those of the imperial provinces belonged to the emperor's separate treasury.

He further bestowed great attention upon the moral and social improvement of the people, as, for example, by encouraging marriage, which had almost fallen into disuse; and nothing in fact was neglected that might increase the material prosperity of his subjects. Notwithstanding the mildness with which Augustus exercised the sovereignty, and notwithstanding his anxiety to conceal the fact that he was the absolute ruler of the empire, conspiracies against his life were formed from time to time, frightened by which he was always on his guard against any unforeseen attack, especially during the latter part of his reign.

Being more concerned about securing the frontiers of his vast empire than about extending them, he proceeded, in B.C. 27, to the north of Spain, for the purpose of subduing the Astures and Cantabri. He carried on the war against them for three years, until in the end those brave mountaineers were compelled to submit, B.C. 24. The Cantabri, however, again revolted, and were not finally subdued till B.C. 19, when they were completely defeated by Agrippa. The Atlantic thus became the frontier of the empire in the west; in Africa the frontiers of Egypt were secured by victories over the Ethiopians and other tribes. In B.C. 20, the Parthian king, fearing a war with Rome, thought it advisable to send back the standards which had fallen into his hands during the campaigns of Crassus and Antony. The existence of several independent tribes in the eastern parts of the Alps was thought to endanger the frontiers of the empire. Accordingly, a war was commenced against them in B.C. 25, which was continued for many years, until, in B.C. 13, they too were completely subdued. The war against these tribes alarmed the Gauls and the inhabitants of Southern Germany; and as bands of the latter nation invaded Gaul, the alarm created at Rome was so great that, in B.C. 16, Augustus himself, at the head of an army, entered Gaul; but after an absence of three years, he returned to Rome, leaving the command of the army on the Rhine to his step-son Drusus, who, until then, had been conducting the war against the Alpine tribes, in conjunction with his brother Tiberius.

There now began a series of dangerous and disastrous wars with the Germans on the east of the Rhine. The object was not so much to make conquests in Germany as to humble and weaken that nation, because it was regarded as a dangerous neighbour of Gaul. When Drusus undertook the command, in B.C. 12, he resolved to conquer the part of Germany between the Rhine and the Elbe. He made several expeditions against that part of Germany, and endeavoured to secure his conquests by building the fortress of Aliso near the sources of the river Lippe. In B.C. 9 he advanced as far as the Elbe, but want of provisions compelled him to return; and on his journey southward he fell from his horse, injuring himself so severely, that a month later he died.

Drusus was succeeded by his brother Tiberius, who, intending to complete what his brother had commenced, crossed the Rhine in B.C. 8; but he was unable to subdue the west of Germany, although he displayed great skill and bravery. After various undertakings by his successor, none of which secured any permanent results, Tiberius, in A.D. 4, resumed the command of the legions on the Rhine; and, partly by successful battles, and partly by prudent negotiations, subdued the country between the Rhine and the Weser, which was then constituted as a Roman province. Peace being thus restored in that part of Germany, Tiberius was called away by a great insurrection of the tribes inhabiting the country between the Danube and the Adriatic. The war against them lasted for two years, until in A.D. 9, the fall of their strong fortress decided the fate of the insurgents.

In the meantime the work of Romanising Western Germany was going on satisfactorily; but the avarice and haughty insolence of the governor Quintilius Varus roused the indignation of the Germans, and a conspiracy was formed against him by *Arminius*, a Cheruscan chief. His tribe was soon joined by others, and Varus, though warned of the danger, allowed himself with a large force to be drawn into an ambuscade, and a battle ensued in the forest of Teutoburg, which lasted for three days, and ended in so complete a defeat of Varus, that the ground was covered with the dead bodies of the Romans. The survivors were sold as slaves, the standards were lost, and Varus in despair threw himself upon his own sword. The Germans looked, and still look, upon Arminius as the great deliverer of their country from the yoke of the Romans. Augustus, on receiving intelligence of this disaster, is said to have been seized with rage and despair. The fortress of Aliso having been destroyed during the war, the Romans, unable to maintain themselves on the eastern bank of the Rhine, henceforth confined themselves to protecting the left bank of the river.

The most important event which marks the reign of Augustus, is the birth of our Lord Jesus Christ. The reign of Augustus, or more correctly the period from the death of Sulla to that of Augustus, forms the golden age of Roman literature. The Latin language then reached its highest development, and the greatest poets, orators, and historians belong to that period. The private life of Augustus was greatly disturbed during his later years by domestic misfortunes. His promising grandsons, Caius and Lucius Cæsar, the sons of his daughter Julia by Agrippa, died in early youth, not without a suspicion that they had been poisoned by their stepmother, Livia, who was anxious to secure the succession to Tiberius, her son by a former marriage. Augustus's daughter Julia, a licentious woman, caused her father so much sorrow and vexation that he found it necessary to banish her. Augustus died on the 19th of August A.D. 14, at Nola, in Campania, whither he had gone to restore his enfeebled health; and immediately afterwards Agrippa Postumus, the last son of Julia by Agrippa, was assassinated to prevent his putting forth any claims against Tiberius. The latter, therefore, now succeeded his step-father without any difficulty, and the imperial dignity remained in the same family until Nero, who was the last of the line, for after his death the imperial throne was generally filled by the choice of the soldiers.

COINS OF THE TRIUMVIRS, M. ANTONIUS AND LEPIDUS.

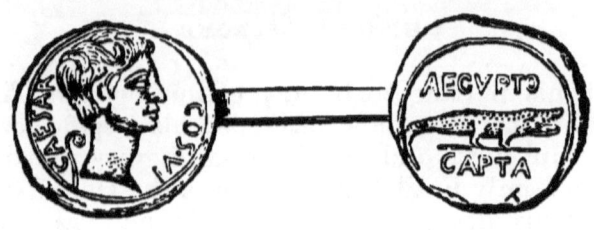

A MEDAL COMMEMORATING THE CONQUEST OF EGYPT.

CHAPTER XIII.

FROM THE DEATH OF AUGUSTUS TO THAT OF NERO.

A.D. 14 TO A.D. 68.

WE have already seen that *Tiberius* greatly distinguished himself in several wars, and nothing is recorded during that period of his life to suggest that he would be the cruel tyrant he turned out to be. During the first six years of his reign, things went on pretty well, at all events, he succeeded in concealing the viciousness of his character. But after the year A.D. 20, when he came under the influence of his friend *Ælius Seianus*, he commenced a series of revolting atrocities. It was on the advice of Seianus that, in A.D. 23, the prætorian cohorts were drawn together into a fortified camp close to Rome, a step which at once changed the government into a military despotism, for henceforth the emperor always had a large body of troops at his command, ready to do his bidding. Hitherto the people had been allowed to assemble in their comitia, and to make laws in the ancient form; but Tiberius abolished those assemblies, transferring their functions to the senate, which, in its servile submissiveness, was ready to do or sanction anything that might please the despot. One of the chief functions of the senate henceforth was to try all cases of high treason against the person of the emperor; and every one was considered guilty of high treason who by speech, deed, or writing, offended the emperor. Such a system raised a host of spies and informers, who stifled every honest expression of opinion, and extinguished the last spark of freedom, while they increased the tyrant's fears and cruelty. During that period the government was virtually in the hands of Seianus; and Tiberius, in order to indulge his sensual and licentious habits free from all restraint, withdrew, in A.D. 26, from the city, and took up his abode in the island of Capreæ, in the Bay of Naples. The period of his absence from Rome was the most terrible part of his reign, for Seianus now ruled without any control whatever. His ambition was to secure the succession to himself, and for this purpose he planned the extermination of the entire family of his sovereign. He had already poisoned Drusus, the only son of Tiberius; and he now sent Agrippina and her three sons into exile, and afterwards got rid of them by starvation or otherwise. *Caius* (afterwards the emperor Caligula), the youngest of the sons of Agrippina by Germanicus, was the only one that escaped. At length, when he thought that all obstacles were removed, he sued for the hand of the widow of Drusus. He had acted in this matter with the greatest caution and secrecy, but it nevertheless reached the ears of Tiberius, who now wrote a letter to the senate accusing Seianus of high treason, and demanding his execution. The order was carried into effect at once, A.D. 31, to the great delight of the Roman people, and Tiberius wreaked his vengeance on all the friends and relatives of Seianus. The experience which the emperor had made with Seianus filled his soul still more with suspicions, and he became still more cruel than before. His health had been ruined by his debauched life; and when he felt his end approaching, though he carefully concealed his condition, he resolved to return to Rome. But he was so universally detested that Macro, the successor of Seianus, in conjunction with

Caius, the son of Agrippina, resolved to get rid of the aged tyrant. While staying at a villa near Cape Misenum, Tiberius fell into a death-like state, and some persons of his suite, believing him to be dead, proclaimed Caius emperor. But Tiberius recovered, and as both Macro and Caius feared his vengeance, they caused him to be suffocated between beds and pillows, A.D. 37.

As regards the affairs of the empire, a great insurrection broke out, in the very year of Tiberius's accession, among the legions on the Rhine and in Pannonia. The soldiers on the Rhine demanded that Germanicus should assume the imperial dignity, instead of Tiberius; but Germanicus was generous enough to quiet the soldiers and decline the offer. The revolt of the troops in Pannonia was quelled by prudent concessions. Germanicus now penetrated into that part of Germany which had been lost through the misconduct of Varus. Arminius again roused his countrymen to a vigorous resistance against the common enemy; but, owing to the superior tactics of the Romans and the prudence of Germanicus, the Germans were defeated in two battles. Tiberius had meanwhile become jealous of the success and popularity of Germanicus, who, in A.D. 16, was recalled, and sent to the East, where he died, at Antioch, A.D. 19. The Germans on the right bank of the Rhine were now left for a time without further molestation. The most memorable event during the reign of Tiberius was the crucifixion of Jesus Christ, according to the common chronology, A.D. 33. We may also mention a fearful earthquake, by which many flourishing cities in Asia were reduced to heaps of ruins; and the great catastrophe at Fidenæ, where a temporary wooden amphitheatre fell in during a gladiatorial exhibition, which had drawn together vast multitudes of people, for no less than 20,000 persons were killed, A.D. 27.

Tiberius was succeeded by *Caius*, commonly called *Caligula*, who reigned from A.D. 37 to A.D. 41. As he resembled his noble-minded father Germanicus in appearance, it was generally hoped that he had also inherited his father's virtues; and during the first eight months of his reign such hopes seemed to be justified. But he was then seized by a sudden illness, from which he indeed recovered, but his conduct was so much altered that henceforth he cannot be regarded in any other light than that of a madman. We need not here enter into the disgusting details of his reign; suffice it to say that he acted as a bloodthirsty tyrant, who took a delight in signing death warrants, and witnessing the agonies of his victims; he squandered the public treasures upon the gratification of his lusts and the erection of absurd buildings; he celebrated ridiculous triumphs over Germans and Britons, whom he had never encountered in battle, and ordered himself to be worshipped as a god. By his excesses he impoverished the provinces, as well as the state treasury; he was a low and vulgar sensualist, whose favourite companions were actors, gladiators, and other persons of the most despised classes. A conspiracy was formed against him as early as A.D. 39, but it was discovered, and its authors were put to death. Another plot was concocted by some officers of the prætorian guards, and in A.D. 41 he was murdered in his own palace, while attending a rehearsal of some actors. His wife and daughters were likewise put to death, and during the tumult, the murderers dragged forth *Claudius*, a son of Drusus and Antonia, who from fear had concealed himself, but was now proclaimed emperor.

The life of Claudius had been spared during the reigns of Tiberius and Caligula, merely because he was despised and looked upon as an idiot. The treatment which he had received from his own family had intimidated him and made him a coward. His favourite pursuits were the study of history and antiquities, and he himself wrote several historical works; but while he occupied himself with such things, his freedmen and favourites governed the empire, exercising unlimited influence over him, and his wife Messalina scorned every law of decency and morality. It was at the instigation of such advisers, that Claudius ordered the execution of some of the best men of the age, and the licentiousness of his court was imitated by the higher classes, especially the ladies. Messalina even went so far as publicly to marry a handsome young Roman. But this step at last opened her husband's eyes, and, frightened by such a shameless proceeding, he ordered her to be put to death, and then married Agrippina, a talented and ambitious woman, but scarcely less licentious than Messalina had been. Her great ambition was to get rid of Claudius's children by Messalina, and to secure the succession to her own son Nero, by a former husband. But when Claudius discovered her scheme, she, in fear of her life, caused him to be poisoned, A.D. 54.

The reign of Claudius, so far as he was not influenced by women and freedmen, was mild and popular. He was fond of building, and executed or completed some very useful works; thus he deepened the harbour at Ostia, and drained Lake Fucinus, by constructing an immense tunnel through which the waters of the lake were led into the river Liris. Notwithstanding the general corruption of the age, the Roman arms under Claudius and his successors gained many a victory abroad. Thus in A.D. 50, a successful war was begun against the Parthians, who had invaded Armenia. In north-western Germany *Corbulo*, one of Claudius's generals, was very successful against the Germans, and might have made that country a Roman province, had he not been ordered by the emperor to confine his operations to the left bank of the Rhine. The reign of Claudius is further remarkable, because it was then that the Romans made permanent conquests in Britain; for in A.D. 43, an army invaded the island, and Claudius, after paying himself a short visit to it, left the command of his troops in the hands of his lieutenants, who continued the war for nine years. It was during this war that *Vespasian* and his son *Titus*, both of whom afterwards became emperors, first distinguished themselves. The south-eastern part of Britain was finally conquered by the Romans, and constituted a Roman province in A.D. 44.

Soon after the murder of Claudius, *Nero*, who was then only seventeen years old, was proclaimed emperor. He had been educated by the philosopher Seneca, and Burrus, an officer of the prætorian guards, and was a young man not without talent; but the corrupt and licentious court, the adulation of the senate, and the servility of the people, exercised their baneful influence. During the first five years of his reign, probably owing to the controlling influence of his teachers, things went on very fairly; but when Nero began to quarrel with his ambitious mother, who not only wanted to interfere in the government, but even threatened to raise Britannicus, a son of Claudius, to the throne, the vicious propensities of Nero burst forth at once. He now first caused the murder of Britannicus, and attempted to drown his mother by means of a boat, constructed in such a manner that it should go to pieces when on the water; but as she saved herself by swimming, he ordered her to be assassinated, and this horrid deed was not censured by either Seneca or Burrus. Under the influence of contemptible women, Nero now hurried from one crime to another; and after the removal of Burrus from the court in A.D. 62, he threw off all restraint: he banished his wife Octavia to a lonely island, where she was murdered, and then married Poppæa Sabina, the adulterous wife of Salvius Otho, who was afterwards raised to the throne. A few years later, a fearful fire broke out at Rome, which lasted for six days, and reduced the greater part of the city to ashes. It was reported that this conflagration was the work of Nero himself, who wished to see a vivid picture of the burning of Troy. But he charged the Christians, who then formed only an obscure sect, with having caused the conflagration, and cruelly persecuted them. It is commonly said that the apostles Peter and Paul suffered martyrdom on that occasion. Nero then ordered the city to be rebuilt with greater magnificence than ever, and for himself he built what was called the "golden house," on the Palatine hill. Although these things could be done only by an arbitrary and despotic ruler, yet the vast Roman populace was kept in good humour by being fed and amused with the plunder of the provinces.

A dangerous conspiracy was formed against Nero, in A.D. 65, by Piso; but it was discovered, and Piso himself, the poet Lucan, and many others, had to pay for the attempt with their lives. Seneca, who was suspected of being an accomplice, put an end to his existence by opening his veins. His next victims were his own wife, Poppæa Sabina, whom he killed in a brutal fit of passion, and Antonia, a daughter of Claudius, whom he ordered to be murdered, because she refused to marry him. Every honest and virtuous person now became an object of fear and hatred to the tyrant. In A.D. 67 Nero went to Greece, and there took part as a player on the lyre in the great national games, distinguishing himself by the grossest follies and cruelties. Soon after his return an insurrection broke out in Gaul, which had been fearfully oppressed by its governors. It was headed by *Julius Vindex*, who offered the sovereignty to *Servius Galba*, the governor of Spain, who was at once proclaimed emperor by the soldiers. The prætorians at Rome, following their example, likewise proclaimed him emperor. Nero, now abandoned by all, took to flight; and on being discovered, inflicted a wound on himself, of which he died, A.D. 68. He was the last survivor of the family of Augustus, and henceforth the prætorians or the legions in the provinces assumed the right of electing the emperor.

During the reign of Nero the Parthians succeeded in gaining possession of Armenia, but Corbulo, a most able general, in a long protracted war, recovered the whole of that country; under his successor, however, it was lost again. Germany was tolerably quiet under Nero; but in Britain a great insurrection broke out, in B.C. 61, in consequence of the fearful rapacity and oppression of the Roman governor. The Britons, headed by their queen, Boadicea, annihilated a whole Roman legion, and destroyed several Roman colonies. But the governor Paulinus, on his return from the island of Mona, where he was engaged at the beginning of the insurrection, defeated the Britons in a great battle, in which 80,000 of them are said to have been killed. Boadicea then put an end to her life, and peace was concluded. Another rebellion, likewise the result of oppression, broke out among the Jews during Nero's stay in Greece. At first the Roman army was defeated, and then the command against them was given to Vespasian, whose exploits there we shall have to notice hereafter.

STATUE OF CALIGULA.

COIN OF CLAUDIUS AND AGRIPPINA.

CHAPTER XIV.

FROM THE DEATH OF NERO TO THAT OF DOMITIAN.

A.D. 68 TO A.D. 96.

Servius Galba, on being informed that he had been proclaimed emperor, and that the choice was sanctioned by the senate, hastened to Rome, accompanied by *Salvius Otho*, the contemptible husband of Poppæa Sabina. The soldiers to whom he owed the throne expected to be richly rewarded by him; but in this they were disappointed; and as he also attempted to restore discipline among them, Salvius Otho formed a conspiracy against him, and he was murdered while crossing the Forum, at the beginning of A.D. 69, after a reign of scarcely eight months; and his son, who had been looked upon as his successor, was likewise killed.

The prætorians now proclaimed Salvius Otho, and their choice was again sanctioned by the senate. He began his reign by punishing some of the persons who had made themselves most obnoxious during the reign of Nero. But he had scarcely entered upon his functions, when he was informed that the legions stationed on the Rhine had conferred the imperial dignity upon their own commander *Vitellius*, who at once sent an army across the Alps; and in a great battle near Bedriacum, gained so decisive a victory over Otho as to drive him to despair and suicide, in April A.D. 69. Otho's army surrendered to Vitellius, who was now the undisputed master of the empire. Vitellius was a man of low tastes, and given to coarse sensual pleasures; he did not trouble himself much about the duties of his office, but allowed the prætorians to act as they pleased with impunity. Such conduct excited general indignation against him; and the legions in several provinces renounced their allegiance. *Vespasian*, who was carrying on the war against the Jews with great success, was proclaimed emperor by the legions that were discontented with the reign of Vitellius. He therefore left the continuation of the siege of Jerusalem to his son *Titus*, and at once prepared for war against Vitellius. Antonius Primus, a staunch supporter of Vespasian, advanced with his army across the Alps, and met that of Vitellius near Bedriacum, where the latter was completely defeated. The victorious army then proceeded to Rome, where a frightful massacre took place in the streets, for Vitellius was forsaken by all parties except the prætorians and the Roman populace, who murdered Sabinus, a brother of Vespasian, in his flight to the Capitol. The splendid Capitoline Temple was destroyed on that occasion by fire. The prætorian camp, in which Vitellius had taken refuge, soon fell into the hands of the partisans of Vespasian; and Vitellius was cruelly murdered in December A.D. 69, after a reign of scarcely eight months.

While these things were going on in Italy, Vespasian was still in the East, and the affairs at Rome were managed by his son *Domitian*, who succeeded in taming the prætorians. The new emperor, who did not arrive at Rome until A.D. 70, was just the man whom Rome required at the time. He immediately set about restoring the discipline among the troops, excluded unworthy men from the senate, watched over the administration of justice, stopped the trials for high treason, and thereby suppressed the detestable class of informers. He was economical in the management of the finances, though he was liberal when money was required for the public good, or for the embellishment of the city. Thus enormous sums were spent upon the restoration of the Capitoline Temple, and on the building of the great amphitheatre, known by the name of the *Colosseum*, which, even in its present ruined state, is one of the grandest structures in Europe. His own example did much to put an end to the licentiousness of the higher classes, and made the senate what it had never been before—an assemblage of the most illustrious men, taken not only from Italy, but from any of the provinces. He was not a man of any great culture, and he had as great a dislike to philosophers as to the extravagant luxuries of his time. In A.D. 74 he expelled all philosophers and astrologers from the city. He hated the Christians, whom he confounded with the Jews, and regarded philosophers as audacious republicans and speculators. In consequence of such one-sided views, several distinguished and noble-minded Stoic philosophers were exiled or put to death.

We have already seen that Vespasian, in A.D. 67, was sent by Nero to conduct the war against the Jews, who had been goaded into a rebellion by the cruelty and insolence of their Roman governor. The Jews fought with the courage of despair, but, after fearful defeats and losses, were confined to the defence of Jerusalem, in which they were besieged by Vespasian. After his elevation to the imperial dignity, the siege of *Jerusalem* was continued by his son Titus. The city suffered terribly from famine and epidemic diseases, multitudes from all parts of the country being crowded together within its walls. It was in vain that Titus offered to spare the people, if they would lay down their arms; and when at length the city was taken, the Jews defended themselves in the Temple, until that venerable and magnificent building became a prey to the flames. The city was then destroyed, and upwards of a million of Jews are said to have perished. The survivors lost their independence for ever; and as they were forbidden to rebuild their city, they dispersed over the whole Roman empire. The triumphal arch of Titus at Rome still bears witness to that terrible catastrophe.

A great insurrection of the *Batavi*, headed by Civilis, had broken out even before Vespasian's arrival in Rome. Their example was followed by other neighbouring tribes, but they were overpowered one after another by the vigour and energy of Cerealis; and in A.D. 70 they had to sue for peace. The year after this, Cerealis was appointed governor of Britain, and was accompanied thither by *Agricola*, the son-in-law of the great historian Tacitus. Six years later, Agricola himself obtained the governorship of Britain, a post which he filled, until A.D. 85, with great benefit to the natives and honour to himself. During this period, all England and the south of Scotland were conquered; and Agricola was the first who, by circumnavigating Britain, established the fact that it was an island.

Towards the end of Vespasian's life a conspiracy was formed against him, for, notwithstanding his general good character, he was occasionally guilty of acts of great cruelty. But the conspiracy was discovered, and its authors were put to death. Soon after this he was taken ill, and died in June A.D. 79.

Vespasian was succeeded by his son, *Titus*, who had latterly governed the empire in conjunction with his father. During his short reign, which lasted only till the month of September A.D. 81, the people at first entertained considerable apprehensions, as he had been guilty of several acts of cruelty; but after his accession he displayed such an amount of kindness and benevolence that he was called by the title of "the love and delight of mankind," and he had plenty of opportunities of showing his benevolence in action. A few months after his accession a fearful eruption of Mount Vesuvius destroyed and buried under burning lava and ashes the towns of Herculaneum, Pompeii, and Stabiæ, and Titus is said to have spent nearly the whole of his property in relieving the sufferings of those who escaped from the catastrophe. The year after, a fire broke out at Rome, which raged for three days, destroying the finest parts of the city; and soon after this calamity a fearful pestilence broke out, carrying off thousands of people in all parts of Italy. The last year of Titus's reign is marked by the inauguration of the Colosseum, which had been commenced by his father, and by the building of the Thermæ, or Baths, which bear his name. After his death, in September A.D. 81, all Romans mourned as over the death of a father. During his reign the frontiers of the empire were not disturbed by foreign aggressions, while Agricola was successfully engaged in the conquest of Britain.

Titus was succeeded by his brother, *Domitian*, who had already become notorious by his tyrannical disposition and many acts of cruelty. At first, however, his conduct was better than his reputation, but after some time he showed himself in his true light as one of the most detestable tyrants that ever disgraced a throne. Hosts of informers again arose, as in the worst days of his predecessors. In order to ingratiate himself with the soldiers, he increased their pay; and to obtain the means for this and his other extravagances, he had recourse to wholesale confiscations, and wealthy persons were treated as criminals solely that the tyrant might gain possession of their property. He scarcely took pleasure in anything except in the fights of gladiators and in torturing his victims, though he was not devoid of some talent, and even dabbled in literature and poetry. In A.D. 83 he undertook an expedition into Germany, and built the frontier wall between the free Germans and those who were subject to the empire. Agricola was pursuing his victorious career in Britain, but as he thereby excited the jealousy of the emperor, he was recalled, A.D. 85. In the year following, the Dacians crossed the Danube, and defeated a Roman army, whereupon Domitian himself took the field against them; but as the German tribes allied with Rome refused to support him, he was obliged to purchase peace of the Dacian king, A.D. 90. Notwithstanding this, he did not scruple on his return to celebrate a triumph over the Dacians, and even assumed the surname of Dacicus. The humiliation to which he was thus obliged to submit rendered him still more ferocious, and he went so far in his madness as to order himself to be worshipped as "lord and god." The most illustrious men were executed for expressing their honest opinions; the philosophers, one of whom was the celebrated *Epictetus*, were expelled; and the Christians, whose numbers were steadily increasing, were persecuted and murdered without mercy. He intended to put his own wife, Domitia, to death; but she, on being informed of it, headed a conspiracy against him, and he was stabbed in his own bedroom by one of her freedmen, in September A.D. 96.

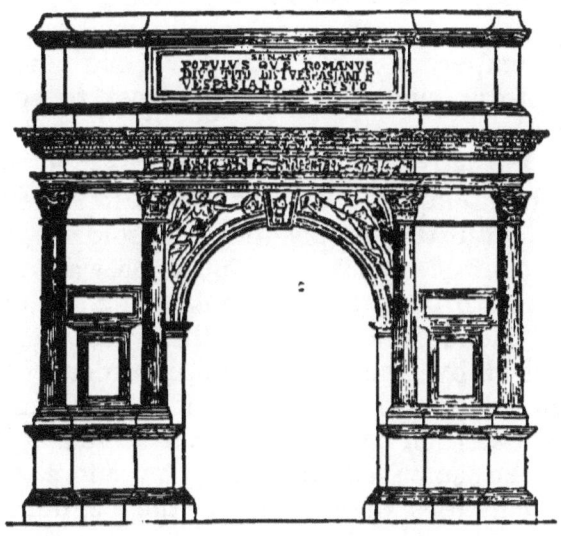

ARCH OF TITUS, RESTORED.

COIN OF HADRIAN.

CHAPTER XV.

FROM THE DEATH OF DOMITIAN TO THAT OF MARCUS AURELIUS.

A.D. 96 TO A.D. 180.

The five emperors who succeeded one another after Domitian form such a strong contrast to some of the wretched tyrants who had preceded them, that the period of their reign is regarded as the happiest in the history of the Roman empire. Immediately after the murder of Domitian, both the people and the soldiers proclaimed *Nerva*, a venerable senator. But as he was not popular with the prætorians, he was obliged to be cautious in punishing offenders and in recalling the men who had been banished by Domitian; and in order to strengthen himself, he adopted *Trajan*, a man of unblemished character, who was then commanding the legions in Germany. However, he survived this step no more than three months, for he died of a fever in the beginning of A.D. 98.

Trajan, having been adopted by Nerva, succeeded him as a matter of course, and arrived at Rome in A.D. 99. He was a native of Spain, and a man of great military talent. His administration of the affairs of the empire met with the approval of the best of his contemporaries.

He first of all suppressed the class of informers, and punished the most turbulent among the prætorians. He then gave back to the senate its ancient powers, promoted commerce by making new roads, canals, and bridges, and by enlarging the port of Centumcellæ. He was the first emperor who promoted the education of children of both sexes, and adorned not only Rome and Italy, but even the provinces, with temples, triumphal arches, and other ornamental buildings.

In Rome he instituted a public library, and laid out a new Forum, in the centre of which rose the famous column which still exists, representing in its bas-relief his own exploits against the Dacians. He was fond of intellectual society, and honoured such men as Tacitus, the historian, and the younger Pliny. His excellent wife, Plotina, and his sister, Marciana, greatly contributed by their example towards the improvement in the conduct of the higher classes.

Trajan deeply felt the humiliation of being obliged to pay to the Dacians the tribute by which Domitian had purchased their peace, and accordingly, in A.D. 100, he proceeded with a large army to Dacia, defeated its king in several battles, took his capital, and at last granted to the king a peace, on condition that a portion of his territory should be ceded to the empire, A.D. 103. But in the year following, the Dacians again rose in arms, and Trajan, having caused a stone bridge to be built over the Danube, marched into Dacia, and pressed the king so hard that, in A.D. 106, he put an end to his own life. Dacia now became a Roman province, and numerous Roman colonies were established in the country, which soon spread Roman civilisation among the Dacians. On his return to Rome, Trajan erected the above-mentioned column.

In A.D. 114, when the Parthians again threatened the frontiers of the empire, Trajan immediately marched against them. In Armenia he was received by the people with open arms, and their country was made a Roman province. He then conquered Mesopotamia, subdued Assyria, and even took the capital of the Parthians. After this he proceeded into Arabia, but being taken ill, he left his legate, Hadrian, in the command of his forces, and was hastening to Rome, when death overtook him, in Cilicia, in August A.D. 117. His remains were carried to Rome, and buried under the column in his own Forum.

Meanwhile a report was spread at Rome, through the empress Plotina, that her husband, during his illness, had adopted *Hadrian*, who happened to be at Antioch, where, accordingly, he was proclaimed. He was a native of Picenum, and connected by marriage with the family of Trajan. He was of a less warlike disposition than his predecessor, and believing that the conquests made in the East would involve the empire in troublesome and dangerous wars, he gave up Mesopotamia and Assyria to the Parthians, and restored Armenia to the rank of an independent kingdom. After settling those affairs in the East, he returned to Rome, A.D. 118, and then marched into Mœsia, but not wishing to make conquests, he concluded peace with the barbarians who had invaded that province. While he was thus engaged abroad, a conspiracy was formed against him by his personal enemies. But the plot was discovered, and its authors severely punished. As his severity created an ill feeling, both in the army and at Rome, he returned to Italy, and did everything to conciliate the senate and the people.

When the frontiers of the empire were thus secured on all sides, he undertook, in A.D. 120, a journey through all the provinces of the empire, during which he visited Gaul, Germany, Britain (the northern part of which he secured against the Scots by a wall from the Tyne to the Solway), Greece, Asia, and Egypt, where his favourite Antinous was accidentally drowned in the Nile. During those journeys he left everywhere memorials of his visits, which were intended to defend and strengthen or embellish cities and provinces; for he was a man of high intellectual culture and noble feelings, though vanity and conceit rendered him easily accessible to flattery.

Towards the end of his life, mistrust and a certain weariness of life sometimes led him to acts of harshness and cruelty. Athens, of which he was particularly fond, was adorned by him with extraordinary splendour; but nowhere did he display his taste for the arts more than in his villa near Tibur, and in his magnificent mausoleum at Rome. A certain kind of literature enjoyed his fostering care, but it was a body without a soul, as it chiefly consisted in grand but hollow phraseology.

In A.D. 133, shortly before Hadrian's return from his travels, a terrible insurrection broke out amongst the Jews, who were exasperated at the establishment of the pagan worship in their country. A desperate war was carried on by them for several years, but in the end they were crushed, and Jerusalem was made a Roman colony, under the name of Ælia Capitolina; the Jews were forbidden to live in the city or its vicinity, and thousands of them were sold as slaves. During the latter year of his reign, Hadrian lived in retirement; his health had been impaired, and he was so tired of life that he made several attempts at suicide, but at last, in July A.D. 138, he died at Baiæ. As Hadrian had no children, he adopted during his illness *Arrius Antoninus*, who in his turn had to adopt *Annius Verus*. During the last three years of his life, Hadrian had committed many acts which excited great discontent, and his adopted son did everything he could to prevent a popular outbreak, whence he obtained the surname of *Pius*—that is, the affectionate or dutiful.

Antoninus Pius, a native of Nemausus in Gaul, owed his adoption by Hadrian solely to his virtues. His reign, from A.D. 138 to A.D. 161, forms the happiest period of the Roman empire. He scrupulously adhered to the principles of his predecessor, and used to say that he would rather save the life of a single citizen than slay a thousand enemies; he was beloved throughout the empire more than any sovereign has ever been beloved either before or since. His whole care was bestowed upon the promotion of the peace and happiness of his people, which he endeavoured to secure by the proper administration of justice, and by educational and charitable institutions. The peace which remained undisturbed during his reign, and his own ardent piety, procured for him the name of a second Numa. The Christians, who were then already very numerous, both at Rome and in the provinces, were not molested in their religious observances. He died, in March A.D. 161, at one of his country villas. Throughout his reign the troops, having been without occupation, had lost their martial spirit, hence when fresh dangers burst in upon the empire under his successors, the armies were not in a condition to meet them.

Antoninus had had two sons, but as they had died before their father, he was succeeded by his adopted son, *Annius Verus*, better known under the name of *Marcus Aurelius*, surnamed the Philosopher, a native of Rome. His education had been conducted with the greatest care, and from his earliest youth he had been distinguished for his love of truth and thirst for knowledge. He was more especially devoted to the doctrines of the Stoic philosophy, which continued to be his favourite study even after he had ascended the imperial throne, though he did not neglect the duties of his high station. But as he was of a delicate constitution, he allowed his adopted brother, *Lucius Verus*, an active young man, to share the sovereign power with him. But Marcus Aurelius did not know the vicious qualities of his brother, who, when abroad at the head of his armies, indulged in every kind of debauchery and voluptuousness. Lucius Verus set out, in A.D. 162, against the Parthians, who now again began to make inroads into the Roman provinces. On his arrival in the East, he gave himself up to his vicious propensities, leaving the management of the war to his lieutenants, who conquered Armenia and Mesopotamia, so that a peace could be concluded with the Parthians, in which they were obliged to cede Mesopotamia to the Romans.

The northern frontiers of the empire were likewise threatened by a number of German and Sarmatian tribes, who intended to invade Italy itself, and had already advanced as far as Aquileia. Soon after Verus's return from the East, he and his brother took the field against the barbarians with such overwhelming forces, as to compel the enemies to retreat before them. Lucius Verus died, A.D. 169, of a fit of apoplexy, and Marcus Aurelius now continued the war with great energy. Several great battles were fought, one on the frozen river Danube; and in another, A.D. 174, the Roman army, being surrounded by the barbarians, was saved only by the bursting forth of a violent storm. This unexpected escape of the Romans filled the enemies with such awe, that they sought for peace, which they obtained on condition that they should withdraw beyond the Danube, A.D. 175.

Soon after this, Marcus Aurelius had to quell an insurrection in the East, headed by Avidius Cassius, who had been instigated by the emperor's own wife, Faustina, a daughter of Antoninus Pius. The emperor succeeded in subduing the insurrection, and treated the ringleaders with unparalleled mercy. While he was engaged in this manner in the East, the Germans and Sarmatians renewed their hostilities; Marcus Aurelius marched against them, and was successful in several battles, but before the war could be brought to a close, he died at Sirmium, in March A.D. 180. His son *Commodus*, who had accompanied him in the war, hastened to purchase peace of the barbarians. Marcus Aurelius, notwithstanding the almost uninterrupted wars which disturbed his reign, found leisure to compose a work called "Meditations," in which we still see him with all his amiable, affectionate, and devout qualities.

COIN OF ANTONINUS PIUS.

COIN OF MARCUS AURELIUS.

CHAPTER XVI.

THE REIGN OF COMMODUS.—CONCLUSION.

A.D. 180 TO A.D. 192.

AFTER having purchased peace of the Germans, Commodus hastened to Rome to give himself up to the pleasures and licentiousness of the capital. He was not yet twenty years old, and had received a careful education; but this, as well as the noble example of his father, was lost upon him. During the first two years, his real character did not appear, and it was hoped that after all he might be better than his reputation. But a conspiracy which his own sister formed against him, in A.D. 183, suddenly produced the most extraordinary change, for the remaining period of his reign was an uninterrupted succession of sanguinary and disgusting excesses. The best friends and advisers of his father were put to death, and Commodus abandoned himself without the slightest sense of shame to the coarsest vices and brutal debaucheries, while the business of the state was left to the lowest and most contemptible creatures. He was a young man of an athletic stature; his great ambition was to distinguish himself as a gladiator, and to be looked upon as a second Hercules. In A.D. 185 he appointed Cleander, one of his favourite freedmen, prefect of the prætorian guards, but this act was so distasteful to the people, that the unworthy favourite was literally torn to pieces by the Roman populace. At the time when Commodus was changing the city into a slaughter-house of the best men of the time, Italy was suffering from plague and famine. In A.D. 192 he formed the design of entering the senate house with a band of gladiators, and murdering the consuls and many other persons of high rank. The list he had drawn up of his intended victims fell into the hands of his mistress Marcia, and as she found her own name among them, she anticipated the plot, and, assisted by several others, she caused the monster to be strangled in his bed, on the last day of the year A.D. 192. His death filled Rome with joy, and the senate cursed his memory; the prætorians alone did not join in the general rejoicing, for upon them the treasures of the empire had been most lavishly squandered by Commodus.

Commodus, throughout his reign, had never troubled himself about the interests of the empire, but its integrity had nevertheless been preserved by the valour and activity of his generals, who successfully warded off or repelled the invasions of the barbarians.

The reign of Commodus forms the real beginning of the decline of the Roman empire, and from this time down to its final overthrow, in A.D. 476, we have, with only very few exceptions, a succession of rulers distinguished for tyranny, baseness, and weakness. The prætorian guards henceforth decided the fate of the empire, and exercised a perfect military despotism. As, however, the legions stationed in the provinces did not always approve of or acquiesce in the sovereign chosen by the prætorians, it repeatedly happened that two or more emperors were proclaimed at the same time in different parts of the empire, which of course led to wars among the rival sovereigns. On one occasion, not long after the death of Commodus, the prætorians went so far as to offer the imperial dignity to the highest bidder. The Christians, notwithstanding the fearful persecutions to which they were exposed under some of the successors of Commodus, steadily continued to become more numerous, until in the reign of Constantine (A.D. 306 to A.D. 337), their numbers and their influence were so great, that Christianity could no longer be suppressed, and became the recognised religion of the empire.

It had long been felt that it was difficult to govern the vast empire from Rome as its central point; at length the emperor Theodosius, shortly before his death in A.D. 395, divided the empire into two parts, the western and the eastern, the Adriatic forming the boundary between them. Rome remained the capital of the West, while Byzantium, which had been much enlarged and embellished by Constantine, became the capital of the East, under the name of Constantinople. In less than a hundred years after this division, the Germans and other barbarians, invading not only the provinces of the western empire, such as Gaul, Britain, Spain, and Africa, but Italy itself, reduced the Roman sovereigns to such a state of weakness, that at last, in A.D. 476, Odoacer, a chief of the German tribe of the Heruli, after making himself master of Rome, wrote to the emperor of the East, that Rome no longer required an emperor, and demanded for himself the sovereignty of Italy. Romulus Augustulus, the last emperor, readily resigned his dignity, and spent the remainder of his life in private retirement in Campania. The Eastern or Greek empire continued its existence for nearly a thousand years longer, until, in A.D. 1453, it was conquered and overthrown by the Turks.

The change which had come over the west of Europe during the last century of the empire was immense. The ancient civilisation and the ancient religion had died away, paganism had given way to Christianity, and the Roman provinces and Italy had been overrun and conquered by Teutonic tribes, which established themselves in the conquered countries, formed independent kingdoms, and thus laid the foundations of an entirely new state of things, out of which our modern states and modern civilisation have arisen. The conquerors settling in the various parts of the empire, in the course of time adopted the language, customs, and laws of the Romans, whence the nations of south-western Europe still speak languages which are essentially Latin; and their manners, customs, and even their Christianity, still bear many traces of Roman influence.

COLUMN OF TRAJAN.

CHRONOLOGICAL TABLE.

B.C. 753	Foundation of Rome.
753-716	**Romulus.** Political institutions.
715-672	**Numa Pompilius.** Religious institutions.
672-640	**Tullus Hostilius.** War against Alba. The Horatii and Curiatii. Alba Longa destroyed. Beginnings of the **plebs**.
640-616	**Ancus Marcius.** Formation of the plebeian order by the conquest of Latins. Ostia built.
616-578	**Tarquinius Priscus** attempts reforms, but is thwarted.
578-534	**Servius Tullius.** Organisation of the plebs, and reforms of the constitution.
534-510	**Tarquinius Superbus.**
509	**Establishment of the republic.** First consuls. Conspiracy at Rome. War with Porsenna.
505	War against the Sabines.
501	War with the Latins.
498	T. Larcius, first dictator.
496	**Battle of Lake Regillus**, in which the Latins are defeated.
495	Death of Tarquinius Superbus. Insurrection of the plebs.
494	**Secession of the plebs** to the *Mons Sacer*.
493	Appointment of the **tribunes of the plebs.** The Ædiles. League of Sp. Cassius with the Latins.
491	Coriolanus stirs up the Volscians against Rome.
486	League of Sp. Cassius with the Hernicans. **First attempt at an agrarian law.**
485	Sp. Cassius put to death, and his agrarian law disregarded.
477	Defeat of the Fabii on the Cremera.
473	The tribune Genucius murdered.
471	The tribune Publilius Volero carries several laws to protect the plebs.
462	The tribune C. Terentillus Arsa demands a revision of the laws.
458	The dictator L. Quinctius Cincinnatus defeats the Æquians.
457	The number of tribunes of the plebs is increased to ten.
454	The bill of Terentillus Arsa is at length carried.
451	**The first decemvirate.**
450	**The second decemvirate.** Laws of the Twelve Tables.
449	Secession of the plebs to the *Mons Sacer*. Deposition of the decemviri. Laws of Valerius and Horatius.

CHRONOLOGICAL TABLE.

B.C.	
445	The tribune Canuleius carries a law establishing the *connubium* between patricians and plebeians.
443	**Institution of the censorship.**
440	Famine at Rome. Sp. Maelius assists the poor.
439	Sp. Maelius murdered by Servilius Ahala.
438	**The first military tribunes instead of consuls.**
426	Fidenæ destroyed.
396	**Capture of Veii** by Camillus after a siege of ten years.
391	Camillus goes into exile. The Gauls besiege Clusium.
390	**Battle of the Allia. Rome taken and destroyed by the Gauls.**
384	M. Manlius Capitolinus condemned to death.
383	The Pomptine district assigned to the plebeians.
376	C. Licinius Stolo and L. Sextius bring forward their rogations.
367	**The Licinian rogations are passed after a struggle of nearly ten years.**
366	L. Sextius, the first **plebeian consul.** First appointment of a prætor.
358	T. Manlius Torquatus defeats a gigantic Gaul on the Allia.
356	**The first plebeian dictator, C. Marcius Rutilus.**
351	**The first plebeian censor.**
350	M. Valerius Corvus slays a Gallic chief by the aid of a raven.
343-341	**First war against the Samnites.**
340-338	War against the Latins. Self-sacrifice of P. Decius.
339	**The laws of Q. Publilius Philo.**
338	Final subjugation of Latium.
337	**The first plebeian prætor.**
328	Foundation of the colony of Fregellæ.
326-304	**Second war against the Samnites.**
322	Luceria in Apulia conquered by the Romans.
321	**Defeat of the Romans at Caudium.** Afterwards they gain several victories.
315	War declared against Rome by the Etruscans.
314	Great success of the Romans against Samnium.
312	The Appian road made.
311	War with the Etruscans breaks out.
309	The dictator L. Papirius Cursor defeats the Samnites.
308	The Etruscan towns conclude peace.
306	The Samnites defeated in all directions. Subjugation of the Hernicans.
305	The Samnites, defeated at Bovianum, sue for peace. The Æquians rise, but are completely crushed.
300	The colleges of augurs and pontiffs thrown open to the plebeians by the **Ogulnian law.**
298-290	**Third war against the Samnites.** The Etruscans and Umbrians also rise again.
295	The Romans recover all Lucania. Victory of the Romans at Sentinum in Umbria. Decius Mus.
292	The Samnites totally defeated; their commander Pontius taken.
290	Samnium, and soon after Etruria and Umbria, recognise the supremacy of Rome.
285-282	**War against the Gauls.** Subjugation of the Senones and Boii.

B.C. 282	The Romans relieve Thurii, which is besieged by the Lucanians.
281	**Pyrrhus, king of Epirus, lands in Italy.**
280	The Romans defeated by Pyrrhus near Heracleia.
279	The Romans again defeated by Pyrrhus at Asculum.
278	Truce between the Romans and Pyrrhus, who goes to Sicily.
276	Pyrrhus returns to Italy.
275	**Pyrrhus, defeated at Beneventum, abandons Italy.**
273	Embassy of Ptolemy Philadelphus to Rome.
272	All southern Italy submits to Rome.
271	Rhegium also is recovered by the Romans.
268	**Fourth and last war against the Samnites,** lasts only one year.
264	The Romans ally themselves with the Mamertines of Messana. Peace with Hiero.
264-241	**The first Punic war.**
262	Agrigentum besieged and taken by the Romans.
260	C. Duilius defeats the Carthaginians off Mylæ.
258	Atilius Calatinus carries on the war in Sicily.
256	The Carthaginians defeated off Ecnomus by M. Atilius Regulus, who sails with his fleet to Africa.
255	Success of Regulus in Africa, but he is afterwards defeated by Xanthippus and taken prisoner. Wreck of the Roman fleet on the coast of Sicily.
254	A new fleet is equipped, and Panormus taken.
252	The Roman fleet sails to Africa, but is wrecked on its return.
250	The Carthaginians defeated near Panormus. Regulus sent as ambassador to Rome. Siege of Lilybæum.
249	Defeat of Appius Claudius by land and sea.
247	**Hamilcar** undertakes the command of the Carthaginians.
242	The Romans build a new fleet.
241	C. Lutatius Catulus defeats the Carthaginians off the Ægates insulæ. Peace with Carthage. **Sicily the first Roman province.**
238	Sardinia and Corsica are taken from Carthage.
229	War against the Illyrian pirates. Agrarian law of C. Flaminius. Death of Hamilcar in Spain: he is succeeded by Hasdrubal.
228	Peace with the Illyrians.
226	The Gauls invade Etruria.
225	The Gauls defeated in the battle of Telamon.
224	Reduction of the Boii.
223	C. Flaminius conquers the Insubrians.
222	M. Claudius Marcellus, in the battle of Clastidium, brings the Gallic war to a close. Cremona and Placentia founded.
221	Assassination of Hasdrubal, who is succeeded by **Hannibal.**
219	Second war against the Illyrians, who are conquered by L. Æmilius Paulus. Capture of Saguntum.
218-202	**The second Punic or the Hannibalian war.**
218	The Romans defeated on the **Ticinus** and the **Trebia.** Cn. Cornelius Scipio goes to Spain.
217	Defeat of the Romans on **Lake Trasimenus.**
216	The Romans defeated at **Cannæ.**
215	Losses of Hannibal at Nola and Beneventum. Syracuse revolts from Rome. Treaty of Hannibal with Philip of Macedonia.

CHRONOLOGICAL TABLE. 161

B.C.

215-205	**First war against Macedonia.**
214-212	**Siege and capture of Syracuse** by M. Claudius Marcellus.
212	The two Scipios slain in battle in Spain.
211	The Romans conquer Capua. P. Cornelius Scipio goes to Spain.
210	Scipio takes Carthago Nova in Spain.
209	Tarentum recovered by the Romans. Hasdrubal defeated at Bæcula.
207	**Hasdrubal** goes to Italy, but is defeated and slain on the Metaurus.
205	P. Cornelius Scipio goes to Sicily.
204	Scipio crosses over into Africa.
203	Syphax taken prisoner.
202	Hannibal recalled to Africa, is defeated in the **battle of Zama.**
201	Peace with Carthage ratified at Rome.
200-197	**Second war against Macedonia.**
200-181	War against the Ligurians, Insubrians, and Boians.
198	T. Quinctius Flamininus undertakes the war against Macedonia.
197	Philip defeated in the battle of Cynoscephalæ. Peace between Macedonia and Rome.
196	Flamininus proclaims the independence of Greece.
192	Antiochus, invited by the Ætolians, crosses over into Europe.
191	Antiochus and the Ætolians defeated at Thermopylæ.
190	L. Cornelius Scipio crosses over into Asia, and defeats Antiochus in the **battle of Magnesia.** Peace concluded.
188	Peace with Antiochus ratified at Rome.
183	**Death of Hannibal.**
181-179	War in Spain brought to a close by Tib. Sempronius Gracchus.
171-168	**Third and last Macedonian war.**
168	Battle of Pydna, in which Perseus is defeated. One thousand Achæans sent to Italy.
155	Greek philosophers expelled from Rome.
151	The surviving Achæans return to Greece.
149	Andriscus, a pretender to the throne of Macedonia.
149-146	**The third and last Punic war.**
148	Andriscus is defeated and slain by Q. Cæcilius Metellus.
148-140	War in Spain. Viriathus.
147-146	War against the Achæans.
146	**Destruction of Corinth,** and subjugation of Greece. **Capture and destruction of Carthage.**
143-133	War against the Celtiberians in Spain. Siege of **Numantia.**
141	Peace with Viriathus.
140	Viriathus murdered by hired assassins.
139	The Gabinian law, ordaining vote by ballot at the elections.
137	Final subjugation of the Lusitanians. C. Hostilius Mancinus concludes peace with the Numantines. The Cassian law, ordaining vote by ballot in the courts of law.
134-132	**Servile war in Sicily.**
133	Numantia taken and destroyed. Attalus of Pergamus dies, bequeathing his kingdom to the Roman people. **Tribuneship of Tib. Sempronius Gracchus:** is murdered.
131-130	War against Aristonicus, who claimed the kingdom of Pergamus.

B.C. 126	First conquests of the Romans in Gaul.
123	**Tribuneship of C. Sempronius Gracchus.**
122	Second tribuneship of C. Sempronius Gracchus.
121	Murder of C. Gracchus, and civil bloodshed at Rome.
113	The Cimbri and Teutones begin their migration westward.
111-106	**The Jugurthine war.**
109	Q. Cæcilius Metellus undertakes the command against Jugurtha. **C. Marius.**
107	First consulship of C. Marius, who succeeds Metellus in Africa.
106	Jugurtha taken prisoner by **L. Cornelius Sulla.** Birth of Cicero.
104	Marius appointed to conduct the war against the Cimbri and Teutones.
102	The Cimbri return from Spain, and are joined in Gaul by the Teutones. **Battle of Aquæ Sextiæ,** in which the **Teutones** are defeated.
102-99	Second servile war in Sicily.
101	The **Cimbri** defeated in the **Campi Raudii.**
100	C. Marius consul for the sixth time. The seditious tribune, L. Appuleius Saturninus, and his party besieged in the Capitol, and afterwards put to death.
91	The tribune M. Livius Drusus attempts to confer the franchise upon the Italian allies, but is murdered.
90-88	**The Social or Marsic war.**
90	The Lex Julia confers the franchise on the Latins.
88	The Etruscans and Umbrians obtain the franchise. End of the Social War.
88-84	**First war against Mithridates.** Civil war between **Marius and Sulla.** Marius flees to Africa.
87	Marius returns to Rome. Scenes of horror at Rome.
86	Siege and capture of Athens by Sulla. Marius dies in his seventh consulship.
84	Peace concluded with Mithridates.
83	Sulla returns to Italy, and is successful against his opponents.
83-81	**Second war against Mithridates.**
82	Capture of Præneste. Young Marius kills himself. Battle at the Colline gate. Q. Sertorius goes to Spain. Sulla enters Rome. First proscription. **Sulla dictator.** Political and legal reforms.
79	Sulla lays down his dictatorship, and withdraws to Puteoli.
79-72	**War against Sertorius.**
78	**Death of Sulla.** Commencement of the war against the pirates.
74-64	**Third war against Mithridates.**
74	Sertorius allies himself with Mithridates of Pontus.
73-71	Servile war in Italy. Spartacus.
73	Lucullus defeats Mithridates.
72	Murder of Sertorius at Osca.
71	The slaves defeated by M. Licinius Crassus.
70	**Cn. Pompey consul.** The political reforms of Sulla abolished.
69	Lucullus defeats Tigranes and Mithridates at Tigranocerta.
67	**Cn. Pompey undertakes the war against the pirates.** Lucullus recalled.
66	**Cn. Pompey obtains the command against Mithridates.**

B.C.	
65	Cn. Pompey pursues Mithridates into Albania and Iberia. J. **Cæsar** is curule ædile, and puts himself at the head of the popular party.
63	Mithridates, being conspired against by his own son, takes poison. **Consulship of Cicero. Catilinarian conspiracy.**
62	Cn. Pompey returns to Italy.
61	Cæsar as proprætor in Spain. **P. Clodius.**
59	**J. Cæsar consul.**
58	P. Clodius tribune. Cicero goes into exile. Cæsar proceeds to Gaul.
57	Cicero recalled.
55	Cæsar receives the administration of Gaul for five years more. He crosses the Rhine, and **invades Britain.**
54	Cæsar invades Britain a second time. Death of Julia, Cæsar's daughter.
53	Cæsar again crosses the Rhine. **Crassus defeated in Syria.**
52	General insurrection in Gaul. Fall of Alesia. Pompey for a time sole consul.
51	Cæsar returns to Cisalpine Gaul. Claudius Marcellus proposes measures against Cæsar.
50	Cæsar is called upon to disband his army.
49	**Cæsar crosses the Rubicon.** Pompey and his party flee from Italy. Cæsar in Spain. On his return he is made dictator.
48	Cæsar consul. **Battle of Pharsalus.**
47	Cæsar defeats Pharnaces of Pontus: crosses over into Africa.
46	**Battle of Thapsus**, in which the Pompeians in Africa are defeated. Cæsar reforms the calendar, and goes to Spain against the sons of Pompey.
45	**Battle of Munda:** the Pompeians defeated.
44	**Cæsar murdered.**
43	War of Mutina. The **triumvirate** between Octavianus, Antony, and Lepidus. Proscription. Death of Cicero.
42	**Battles of Philippi.**
41	**War of Perusia.**
40	Capture and destruction of Perusia. War with the Parthians.
39	Peace of Misenum with Sext. Pompeius.
38-36	**War against Sext. Pompeius.**
36	Sext. Pompeius defeated in the battle of Mylæ. Lepidus deposed. Antony sustains great loss against the Parthians.
34	Antony conquers Armenia, and gives it to Cleopatra.
32	War declared against the queen of Egypt.
31	**Battle of Actium.**
30	Death of Antony and Cleopatra.
29	Octavianus returns to Rome.
27	Octavianus receives the title of **Augustus and Imperator.** Division of the provinces. Augustus goes to Spain.
25-13	War against the Alpine tribes.
24	Augustus returns from Spain.
23	Augustus obtains the tribunician power for life.
20	The Parthians send back the Roman standards.
19	The Cantabri finally subdued by Agrippa.
16-13	Augustus in Gaul, to protect its eastern frontiers.

CHRONOLOGICAL TABLE.

B.C. 12	Death of Lepidus and Agrippa.
12-9	Drusus has the command against the Germans.
8-6	Tiberius succeeds Drusus against the Germans.
6	Domitius Ahenobarbus takes the command against the Germans.
5 or 4	**Birth of Jesus Christ.**
A.D. 4	Tiberius resumes the war against the Germans.
5	Western Germany a Roman province.
6-9	War against the revolted Dalmatians and Pannonians.
9	Defeat of Varus.
14	**Death of Augustus.**
14-37	Reign of **Tiberius**.
14	Revolt of the legions in Germany and Pannonia.
16	Germanicus recalled from Germany.
19	Germanicus dies in Syria.
20	Ælius Seianus guides the counsels of Tiberius.
23	The *castra prætoria* established near Rome. Drusus, son of Tiberius poisoned.
26	Tiberius withdraws to Capreæ.
31	Execution of Ælius Seianus.
33	Crucifixion of Jesus Christ.
37	Tiberius murdered by suffocation.
37-41	Reign of **Caligula**.
39	A conspiracy formed against Caligula.
41	Caligula murdered.
41-54	Reign of **Claudius**.
43	Commencement of permanent conquests in Britain.
50	Successful war against the Parthians.
51	The south-eastern part of Britain a Roman province.
54-68	Reign of **Nero**.
54	Corbulo drives the Parthians from Armenia.
61	Insurrection in Britain under Boadicea.
62	Nero banishes Octavia. Burrus put to death.
64	Great fire at Rome.
65	Seneca the philosopher and Lucan the poet put to death.
66	Tiridates recognised as king of Armenia.
67	Nero goes to Greece. Insurrection of the Jews. Vespasian conducts the war against them.
68-69	**Servius Galba**, is murdered.
69	**Salvius Otho**, defeated at Bedriacum, kills himself.
69	**Vitellius**, is murdered in the prætorian camp.
69-79	**Vespasian**. The siege of Jerusalem is left to Titus.
70	Vespasian arrives at Rome. Capture and destruction of Jerusalem. Insurrection of Claudius Civilis and the Batavi.
71	Petilius Cerealis, governor of Britain, is accompanied by Agricola.
74	Philosophers expelled from Rome.
77-85	Agricola governor of Britain.
79-81	Reign of **Titus**.
79	First recorded eruption of Vesuvius, and destruction of Herculaneum, Pompeii, and Stabiæ.
80	Great fire at Rome. Completion of the Colosseum.
81-96	Reign of **Domitian**.
83	Domitian undertakes an expedition against the Chatti.

CHRONOLOGICAL TABLE.

A.D.	
84	Agricola defeats the Caledonians under Galgacus.
86	The Dacians make war against the Romans.
90	Domitian purchases peace of the Dacians.
96-98	Reign of **Nerva**.
98-117	Reign of **Trajan**.
100	Trajan sets out against the Dacians.
103	Peace with the Dacians.
104-106	Second Dacian war, at the end of which Dacia becomes a Roman province.
114	War against the Parthians.
115	Armenia a Roman province.
117-138	Reign of **Hadrian**; he makes the Euphrates the boundary in the East.
118	Hadrian returns to Rome from the East. War against the Sarmatians. A conspiracy against him suppressed.
120	Hadrian travels through the provinces of the empire.
131-136	War against the Jews.
138-161	Reign of **Antoninus Pius**. Peace throughout the empire.
161-180	Reign of **M. Aurelius**.
162	L. Verus goes to the East against the Parthians.
166	Peace concluded with the Parthians.
167	War against the Marcomanni and Quadi.
169	Death of L. Verus.
175	Peace with the Marcomanni concluded. Revolt of Avidius Cassius in the East.
178	Renewal of the war against the Marcomanni.
180-192	Reign of **Commodus**.
180	Commodus purchases peace of the Marcomanni.
183	Conspiracy against Commodus headed by his sister Lucilla.
184	War against the Caledonians terminated.
185	Perennis recalled from Britain, and put to death.
306-337	Reign of Constantine.
476	Deposition of the last Roman emperor.

www.ingramcontent.com/pod-product-compliance
Lightning Source LLC
Chambersburg PA
CBHW030254170426
43202CB00009B/737